PREGNANT?
ADOPTION IS AN OPTION

Other Books by Jeanne Warren Lindsay:

Teenage Couples—Expectations and Reality

Teenage Couples—Caring, Commitment and Change:
How to Build a Relationship that Lasts

Teenage Couples—Coping with Reality: Dealing with Money,
In-Laws, Babies and Other Details of Daily Life

Teens Parenting—Your Baby's First Year

Teens Parenting—The Challenge of Toddlers

Teen Dads: Rights, Responsibilities and Joys

Do I Have a Daddy? A Story About a Single-Parent Child

School-Age Parents: Challenge of Three-Generation Living

Parents, Pregnant Teens and the Adoption Option

Open Adoption: A Caring Option

By Jeanne Lindsay and Jean Brunelli:

Teens Parenting—Your Pregnancy and Newborn Journey
(Available in "regular" [RL 6],
Easier Reading [RL 3], and Spanish editions.)

By Jeanne Lindsay and Sally McCullough:

Teens Parenting—Discipline from Birth to Three

By Jeanne Lindsay and Sharon Rodine:

Teen Pregnancy Challenge, Book One: Strategies for Change

Teen Pregnancy Challenge, Book Two: Programs for Kids

By Jeanne Lindsay and Catherine Monserrat:

Adoption Awareness: A Guide for Teachers,
Counselors, Nurses and Caring Others

Pregnant?
Adoption
Is an Option

Making an Adoption Plan
for a Child

Jeanne Warren Lindsay, MA, CFCS

Illustrated by Jami Moffett

Morning
Glory
Press

Buena Park, California

Copyright © 1997 by Jeanne Warren Lindsay

All Rights Reserved

Library of Congress Cataloging-in-Publication Data
Lindsay, Jeanne Warren.
   Pregnant? Adoption Is an Option : Making an Adoption Plan for a
Child / Jeanne Warren Lindsay : illustrated by Jami Moffett.
      p. cm.
   Includes bibliographical references (p.   ) and index.
   Summary: Discusses adoption as an option for pregnant young
women who do not have the resources to parent well, exploring how
such a solution could affect the birthmother, the child, and the father.
   ISBN 1-885356-09-9 (Hardcover). -- ISBN 1-885356-08-0
(Quality paper)
    1. Adoption--United States--Juvenile literature.   2. Teenage
pregnancy--United States--Juvenile literature.   3. Teenage mothers--
United States--Juvenile literature.   [1. Adoption. 2. Pregnancy.
   3. Teenage mothers.]   I. Title.
HV875.L47   1996
362.7'34--dc20   96-31589
                                                              CIP
                                                              AC

MORNING GLORY PRESS, INC.
6595 San Haroldo Way   Buena Park, CA 90620-3748
      (714) 828-1998   FAX (714) 828-2049
   Printed and bound in the United States of America

CONTENTS

Does pregnancy necessarily mean parenthood? If the pregnancy continues, many people assume parenting is the only rational, normal follow-up.

The other choice, adoption, is often ignored. How could a mother allow someone else to rear her child? How can a father deliberately turn his child over to another family to parent?

Pregnant? Adoption Is an Option is for those pregnant women and couples who, for emotional, financial, or other reasons wonder if now is the time to be parenting. Many of them, probably most, may be opposed to the old style of adoption in which the birthparents appeared only in the shadows as their child was whisked away and turned over to another family. And as far as the child and the adoptive parents were concerned, the birthparents were likely to remain in those shadows, always out of sight, perhaps out of mind.

Adoption today can be, and often is, quite different. No longer must the birthparents ignore their responsibility for their child's welfare by simply turning him over to strangers.

Today, they realize they need to make a well-thought-out
adoption plan, carefully choose the family for their child, and
perhaps remain in contact with the child and her adoptive
family throughout the coming years.

Public opinion changes slowly. Bring up the subject of
adoption in a social setting, as I often do, and you still hear
mostly about the waiting couples. They can't get a child, or if
they do, "the birthmother will probably come back and disrupt
all our lives." I hear comments inferring that birthmothers
tend to be druggies with no sense of responsibility or de-
cency—and the birthfather, well . . . let's forget about him
whenever possible.

Reality, of course, is quite different. It takes a great deal of
love, concern, and *strength* to make an adoption plan for
one's child and carry out that plan. It also takes a real sense of
responsibility to choose an adoptive family suitable for this
beloved child.

Pregnant? Adoption Is an Option is written expressly to
birthparents. It is also an effort to help others understand
better the loving realities of adoption as it is practiced today.

Jeanne Warren Lindsay
September, 1996

The word adoption brings forth many images and feelings
in our society. We think of orphans in Russia and China;
crack babies in hospitals all over the United States; couples
advertising in newspapers across our country for the chance to
parent; the big business of adoption; and the high profile cases
of Baby Jessica and Baby Richard. We see the movies at-
tempting to address the stereotypes of adoption with such
titles as "Problem Child"; "Losing Isaiah"; "Immediate
Family"; and "Flirting with Disaster." The TV show, "Second
Noah," has given us a weekly glimpse of special needs and
transracial adoptions.

The many celebrities adopting has moved adoption out of
the shadows as a high profile form of family building. What
we still struggle with in our society is the concept of birthfamily and the possibility of ongoing relationships between
the birth and adoptive families over the years. Jeanne Warren
Lindsay has been one of the leaders of our consciousness-
raising about the birthfamily and open adoption choices. She
has authored many fine books and made public presentations

on these topics. This latest publication, *Pregnant? Adoption Is an Option,* continues this fine tradition.

My experience as an adoptive mother and as an adoption professional for more than three decades has shown me clearly that adoption works, but that it creates unnecessary pain, loss, and mystery. I have never worked with a prospective birthparent who didn't ask at some time during their counseling, "Will my child hate me for this decision?" They want to know if they will be notified if something happens to their child or if they will be called if their child needs something. They are looking for validation that they made the right choice.

Many adoptive parents want to know what happened to the birthfamily. They worry about running into a member of the birthfamily unaware of who they are, or find themselves fumbling for answers to the questions their children ask as they grow. They realize that the medical information they were given for the child grows old too soon or is incomplete.

Adoptees have a need to know more about themselves as they grow. Who do I look like? Where do I come from? Do I have brothers and sisters out there in the world? Are my birthparents okay?

We have certainly learned that the fact of the relinquishment and the fact of the adoption are two different issues in the adoptee psyche; one does not cancel the other out. Both need to be acknowledged, discussed, and demystified.

Teen parents have particular needs that Jeanne Warren Lindsay acknowledges well in her large body of published works. Teens are forced, by this unplanned pregnancy, to confront many of their own appropriate developmental stages. Teens, by the very fact that they are teens, are present-focused, self-involved, and living in two worlds of dependence and bidding for independence. They generally don't trust adult authority figures, and are still usually relying on their parents to help them with the larger decisions of life.

However, in relation to their baby, teens must make a present-focused as well as a later-focused decision. They must deal with lawyers, social workers, medical personnel, and court representatives. They must think of their baby separate from themselves, deal with prospective adoptive parents, and with issues that may run counter to their cultural, family, and religious community.

Most certainly their extended family will be having a lot of their own feelings in relation to the new relative on the way into the world. Birthgrandparents may grieve profoundly the arrival of this, perhaps first, grandchild. The teen parents may seem to breeze through all this, only to do their grief work years later. All this points to the importance of adoptive parents who can honor the whole birthfamily and see the need to stay in touch with them over time.

Attitudes have changed about open adoption in the past few years in many parts of the country, although there are still large areas where open adoption is an enigma. People seem less angry and fearful when discussing the birthfamilies of their children. Generally, the questions are less about "Why recognize the birthfamily as important to a child?" but more of "How do we do this so that it will be good for our child?"

Ongoing research and anecdotal material has shown us that open adoption is not hurting the children and, indeed, seems to aid the child in growing a healthy identity and in feeling better about the adoption without having to deal with so much mystery in their lives. It creates adoption by addition instead of subtraction. You don't have to lose a family to gain more family.

We have certainly learned that open adoption does not make adoption easier for anyone. It does seem to place squarely on the shoulders of the adults involved the job of building connections between families and of nurturing those connections over time. This can insure an intact heritage for the child and offer less work for the adoptee over time.

It does not take away the grief of the birthfamily; the fears of the adoptive family; the overall bittersweet aspects of adoption. It does, however, give all the parties involved a chance to work through these issues; have a sense of validation of their decisions; play a role in the child's life, albeit a different role than they might have played; and a chance to take the high moral ground.

A colleague of mine, Dr. Randolph Severson, has written that adoptive families are built through the heart and spirit. I do believe that open adoption allows us to take the high moral ground. We can honor the spiritual connection between the birth and adoptive family that is created through the marriage that occurs between the adoptee's physical birth and genetic heritage from one family and the emotional and spiritual birth from the adoptive family.

The type of "entrustment ceremonies" that take place today that allow for a safe transition emotionally for the child from one family to another is an honoring of this expanded and spiritually based form of family building. When people ask me today why they should participate in a more open adoption, I say it is based on:

• *Do unto others as we would have them do unto us.*

How many of us could see a relative disappear from our family circle and not care where they went or how they were doing over time? Even if one relative couldn't care for a child at a certain point in time, wouldn't we care as grandparents, aunts, uncles, or siblings?

• *The Ten Commandments.*

Adoption is a child welfare issue. We cannot "steal" children or "covet" other people's children because of infertility. We need to be "honest" about our fears and sadness, but do the right thing in "honoring" the *mothers and fathers* of our children by adoption.

Adoptive parents will feel much more entitled to parent

their children by adoption if they are blessed to do so by the birthfamily. Secrets held in a family over time create lies and family dysfunction. For adoption to be healthy and joy-filled, it needs to be handled in an honest fashion. Both birth and adoptive families tell me that by honoring each other for the roles they share in a child's life, they find adoption easier and quite natural over time.

Adoptive and birthfamilies are forming expanded kinship circles, circles that acknowledge both kinship by blood and kinship by caring. Since an unprecedented number of children growing up in this country are being raised in households where the children are not genetically related to both parents (adoption, foster care, step families, blended families, surrogate births, egg donor births, donor insemination), it is incumbent upon us to redefine family in America to match the reality. These are solid avenues of family growth, but they do cause us to recognize additional people in reference to our children.

The question becomes not "Who does this child belong to?" but, "Who belongs to this child?" Adoptive and birth families are leading the way through open adoptions in creating this expanded vision of family growth and definition. It is honest, loving, respectful, and the right thing to do for our children.

Sharon Kaplan Roszia
Co-Author, *The Open Adoption Experience*

ACKNOWLEDGMENTS

The birthparents who shared their stories of untimely pregnancy, adoption planning, choosing another family for their child, and the grief they faced as their beloved child was placed with adoptive parents—these are the people on whom this book depended. I learned so much from them all.

While their quotes are given under assumed names, most of them gave me permission to thank them here, using their real names: Aleisa Koester, Amber Braden, Anne Melvin, Ashley White, Beth Talbot and Paul Edwards, Detra Dudley, Erin Hauck, Eunice McClymont, Eva Arizmendi, Jacqueline Clemons, Jennifer Hurley, Jeremiah Woodcock, Jessica Scott-Nairns, Jim and Krista Beirne, Laura Nelson, Lori Bolduc, Laurie Emmer, Lisa Bentson, Marianne Satinsky, Megan Mayer, Michelle Brummitt, Michelle Andrea Drake, Michelle Proffit, Mike Stallings, P. J. Cullen, Paula Dixon, Rachel Waldorf, Sandra Andreola, Sarah Koester, Shane Elkin, Susannah Oh, Suzanne Haag, Tania Bouillet, and Tricia Hackett.

Several adoptive parents, adoptees, and birthgrandparents

also shared their stories including Kevin and Diane Boys,
Julie George, Ann Marie Mitroff and Norman Groner, Anita
Culbertson, Mary White, Terry Engstrom, and Casey
Borgeson. I thank each one.

Sharon Kaplan Roszia's Foreword adds a great deal to this
book and I am grateful. I also appreciate all those others who
shared their expertise, referred individuals for interviewing,
and/or critiqued the manuscript: Sharon Roszia, Genie
Wheeler, Janet Fish, Sarah Jensen, Shane Elkin, Enid Callen,
Deane Borgeson, Carole Adlard, Nancy Johnson, Deborah
Crouse Cobb, Diane Woodcock, Susanne Oh, Kevin and
Diane Boys, Wendy Heiser, and Erin B. Lindsay.

Jami Moffett's beautiful and sensitive illustrations catch
the essence of *Pregnant? Adoption Is an Option,* and Tim
Rinker's cover design adds to the book's appeal. I truly enjoy
working with these talented people.

Carole Blum and Karen Blake helped with the proof-
reading and kept the office going as usual while this book was
being written. And Bob, as always, shopped, kept the comput-
ers running, and, most important, encouraged and loved me. I
appreciate him most of all.

Jeanne Lindsay

To the birthparents
who share so freely on these pages
their stories of love, concern, and caring
for their children.

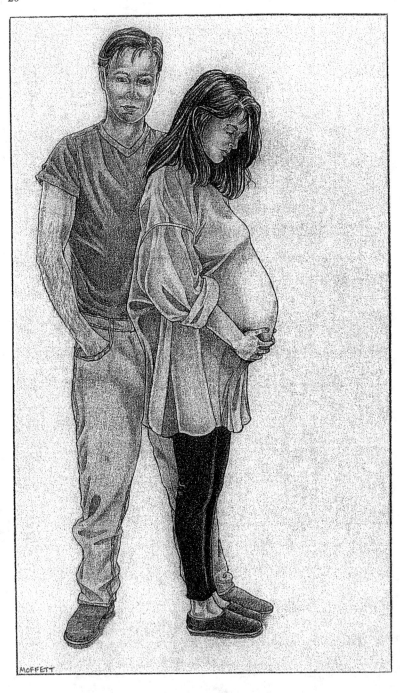

INTRODUCTION

Adoption begins with the birthparents. If you're pregnant, or your partner is, you may not feel entirely ready to parent at this time. If you consider an adoption plan, know right off that *you* are where it begins. Not the adoptive parents.

It is *you* who must choose the best possible home and family for your child. You may choose yourself. Or you may carefully and lovingly select an adoptive family. It is *your* responsibility.

Adoption planning in the United States has changed greatly from the secretive affair of a generation ago. No longer must birthparents resign themselves to the heartbreak of never seeing their child again if s/he is placed with another family. Openness is preferred by many birth and adoptive families.

My idea about adoption was that you throw your kid into some black hole and you never see him again. Then I talked to Sarah (counselor) *and my mom, and my views totally changed.*

Eleyna

No longer must birthparents hand their beloved child over
to complete strangers, people about whom they know very
little. If they wish, birthparents today can choose carefully and
responsibly the adoptive family they feel would be best for
their child. They may negotiate a plan of visiting their child
periodically. In fact, in some open adoptions, the adoptive
family considers the birthparents an important part of their
extended family.

In legal adoption, the adoptive family still rears the child.
They are in charge once the adoption is finalized. That has not
changed. The love that child receives, however, need not be
limited, and birthparents can be part of that circle of love.

Pregnant? Adoption Is an Option looks at adoption from
the birthparents' perspective. If one doesn't have the resources to parent well, or simply is not ready for the life-long
impact of parenthood, adoption *is* an option. For many people,
an untimely pregnancy means a choice between abortion and
parenting. If abortion is unacceptable, parenthood *must*
follow.

This book looks at the third choice—not in a starry-eyed
"such a wonderful decision" manner, but rather, with a
realistic approach to what is.

These chapters are written with the understanding that
many birthmothers are alienated from their child's father—
and with the understanding that each child has two parents. In
the 35 adoptions covered in these interviews, thirteen of the
birthfathers were actively involved in the adoption decision.
All birthfathers, of course, either signed the adoption papers
or had their rights terminated by the court.

Birthfathers, like birthmothers, are caring, concerned
people who also want their child to have the best possible life.
They, too, have the responsibility to plan for their child's
future, whether with the birthparents or carefully selected
adoptive parents. Stressed here is the need to involve
birthfathers in adoption planning and in counseling services.

Nature or Nurture?

It's an age-old question. Which influences a child more, nature (genetic heritage) or nurture (environment)? The answer, of course, is "Both." For many people, nature and nurture are entwined in the same set of parents. For adoptees, the birthparents provide the *nature,* and the adoptive parents, the *nurture.*

Obviously, both are important. Closed, confidential adoption denies the child's genetic heritage, and many of us are realizing this is not a rational, caring approach. Those who suggest that the adopted child will be confused knowing two sets of parents ignore an important reality: secrets are much more confusing, secrets that may be defined later as lies by a child denied information about and access to her birthparents.

Children are able to accept their realities when those realities are presented in an honest, caring, and loving fashion. For many young adoptees today, those realities mean an extended family consisting of birth and adoptive family members.

A child defined adoption as moving from one mother's tummy to another mother's heart. A beautiful description of adoption for the adoptive family, it is also a low-key expression of the poignancy and the pain almost inevitably experienced by the birthparents. What must it feel like to birthparents to have their child move to someone else's heart?

Special Terms for Adoption

Birthmother, birthfather, birthparents, and *birthgrandparents* refer to the family into which a child is born. The terms as used here mean members of the birthfamily of a child who has been released for adoption to another family.

Sometimes the term "natural parent" has been used to refer to the parent who gave birth to a baby, then released that baby for adoption. Some people feel this implies the adoptive parents must be "unnatural." To avoid this connotation, *birthparent* is the preferred term.

Technically, the word *relinquishment* refers to the birthparents legally signing over to an adoption agency (giving up their rights to) their child. The agency then places the child with its adoptive family. Until the child is placed, the agency, not the birthparents, has custody of the child.

Consent to adopt is the term used to refer to birthparents legally releasing their child directly to its adoptive parents as is done in independent adoption.

Throughout this book, the terms *relinquish, release,* and *consent to adopt* are used interchangeably. Each refers to the legal act of releasing one's birthchild for adoption by another family. *Placement* or *to place* in this book denotes the act of handing the child over to the adoptive family.

In the past, the phrase, "giving up for adoption," was often used. Today, *making an adoption plan* is preferred. These words imply that the birthparents are involved in the adoption process, as normally happens in open adoption. They may select the adoptive parents and help plan future contact.

Open adoption to some people means simply some form of communication between birth and adoptive parents. For this book, open adoption means the birthparents and the adoptive parents meet and have the opportunity to establish an on-going relationship with each other, if either party wishes to do so. The adoptive parents are the "real" parents because they are responsible for the child in the practical day to day, year by year sense. The birthparents may visit occasionally, or the families may form a true extended family relationship.

The term *facilitator* refers to someone who can help you make and carry out an adoption plan. This may be a counselor or social worker in a licensed adoption agency or adoption service. An adoption facilitator may also be an attorney, doctor, or independent adoption practitioner.

The term *mediator* is also used, meaning a third party who assists in arranging an adoption and setting up a contact agreement between the birth and the adoptive parents. For guidelines on choosing an adoption facilitator or mediator, see pages 114-116.

Birthparents Share Experiences

For this book, thirty-nine birthparents shared their experiences, their beliefs, and their philosophies concerning adoption. Interviews were conducted in 1996. Most of the birthparents quoted here delivered healthy, first-born babies who were placed immediately with their adoptive parents. Several, however, placed under different circumstances.

Three were already parenting other children when they made an adoption plan for a newborn. One couple placed an infant they had parented the first 21/2 months after birth. One birthmother made the heartbreaking decision to place her four-year-old son with an adoptive family.

Six adoptive parents, two birthgrandmothers, and two adoptees also shared their experiences with open adoption for this book. Chapter 14 is an account of one adoption from the viewpoints of the birthmother and the adoptive parents. It is an inspiring story of two families going into an extended family relationship because of the love they share for their child—and their resulting love for each other.

All names of birthparents, adoptees, and adoptive parents quoted on these pages have been changed. Included in the 39 birthparent interviewees were fifteen aged 14-17; twenty, 19-24; and four, 25 or older. Thirty-four were Caucasian; three, African American; and two, Hispanic.

The interviews cover 35 adoption placements. Both the birthmother and birthfather were interviewed concerning four of the placements. One birthmother placed one infant, then a second newborn three years later.

Two days after one newborn was placed with an adoptive couple, he was returned to the birthmother because the birthfather refused to sign the adoption papers. The mother is now parenting the child.

Birthparents — Interview Data

BIRTHMOTHERS:

Alexis: W; 18; NB 41/2 yr. ago; BF not inv.; contact—open.

Alvera: B; 25; NB 4 yr. ago; 1 other child; BF not inv.; contact—facilitator.

Annette: H; 16; 4-yr.-old 2 yr. ago; BF not inv.; contact—open.

April: W; 21; NB 21/2 yr. ago; BF inv.; contact—open.

Aryanna: W; 27; NB 2 yr. ago; parenting 2 sons; contact—through facilitator.

Carmen: W; 15; NB 9 months ago; BF not inv.; contact—open.

Cassandra: W; 16; NB 8 months ago; reclaimed 2 days later (BF didn't sign).

Cecelia: W; 20; NB 5 yr. ago; BF not inv.; contact—open at first, now closed.

Cerissa: W; 15; NB 6 yr. ago; BF inv.; contact—through agency.

Danielle: W; 21; NB 4 months ago; BF (**Derek**) inv.; contact—open.

Eleyna: W; 15; NB 3 months ago; BF not inv.; contact—open.

Emily: W; 2 adoptions—22, 25; NB 41/2 yr., 11/2 yr. ago; BF not inv.;
   contact—#1, open, closed in 5 months; #2, open.

Erica: W; 18; NB 4 yr. ago; BF inv.; contact—through adoption facilitator.

Heather: W; 30; NB 4 months ago; BF not inv.; contact—through agency.

Jazmin: H; 20; NB 7 yr. ago; BF not inv.; contact—through agency.

Julie: W; 27; NB 18 months ago; BF not inv.; contact—open.

Katelynn: W; 20; NB 3 yr. ago; BF inv.; contact—through adoption facilitator.

Kathleen: W; 17; NB 7 yr. ago; BF (**Nick**) inv.; contact—through agency.

Kernisha: W; 19; NB 1 month ago; BF not inv.; contact—open.

La Tasha: W; 16; NB twins 11/2 yr. ago; BF not inv.; contact—facilitator.

Lissette: W; 17; NB 7 yr. ago; BF not inv.; contact—through agency.

Loryna: W; 17; NB 2 yr. ago; BF not inv.; contact—through agency.

Maggie: W; 18; NB 6 yr. ago; BF not inv.; contact—through agency.

Maya: W; 18; NB 4 yr. ago; BF not inv.; Closed 10 yr.; reunited 4 yr. ago.

Nita: W; 16; 21/2-month-old 3 months ago; BF (**Joe**) inv.; contact—agency.

Pati: W; 21; NB 1 yr. ago; BF not inv.; contact—through agency.

Rita: W; 18; NB 6 yr. ago; BF (**David**) inv.; contact—open.

Sabrina: W; 19; NB 2 yr. ago; BF inv. contact—open.

Sonia: W; 17; NB 3 yr. ago; BF not inv.; contact—open.

Sunisha: W; 18; NB 6 weeks ago; BF inv.; contact—open.

Tatum: B; 15; NB 10 yr. ago; BF deceased; contact—through agency.

Taylor: W; 18; NB 7 yr. ago; BF inv.; contact—through agency, now closed.

Veronica: W; 17; NB 17 yr. ago; BF not inv.; closed 17 yrs.; reunited 1 yr.

Yvette: B; 17; NB 4 yr. ago; BF inv.; contact—through agency.

BIRTHFATHERS:

Derek: W; 23; NB 4 months ago; birthmother—**Danielle;** contact—open.

David: W; 23; NB 6 yr. ago; birthmother—**Rita;** contact—open.

Joe: W; 16; 21/2 months ago; birthmother—**Nita;** contact—through agency.

Nick: W; 19; NB 7 yr. ago; birthmother—**Kathleen;** contact—through agency.

Erik: W; 22; NB 16 yr. ago; contact—closed.

In 13 cases, contact between the birth and adoptive parents is direct and continuing. All but three of these placements occurred less than three years ago. Sixteen of the birthparents have contact with the adoptive family through the adoption agency (11) or independent adoption facilitator (5). Ten of these placements occurred *more* than three years ago.

Three placements were open through the agency (one) or facilitator (two) at first, but the adoptive parents have since stopped all contact with the birthparents. In most states, the birthparents have no legal recourse if communication from the adoptive parents stops after the adoption is finalized.

These birthparents are, of course, sadly disappointed. They talked of their concern for their children, and at the same time, reiterated their belief that the adoption was the best plan *given the situation.* They also offer pointers on developing a relationship with adoptive parents that will make loss of contact less likely.

Three adoptions, occurring 14, 16, and 18 years ago, were closed from the beginning. In two, the birthchild has been reunited with the birthparent(s).

If you'd like to know something about the specific person being quoted, you can check the chart on the opposite page. The following abbreviations are used:

Ethnicity: W=Caucasian; B=African American; H=Hispanic.

Age: refers to birthparent's age at time child was released.

Placement data:
  Age of child: NB=Newborn; otherwise age is given in months or years.
  "__ **yr. ago":** Time between placement and interview. If birthmother was parenting other children at time of placement, that information is noted.

BF inv./BF not inv.: Birthfather involved/not involved in the adoption decision. All birthfathers either signed for the adoption, or rights were removed by the court.

Contact between birthparents and adoptive parents:
   Open: Open contact between birth and adoptive families.
   Agency: Contact between families through agency only.
   Facilitator: Contact through facilitator only.
   Closed: No contact between families.

These birthparents talked about the shock of the (usually) unexpected pregnancy and of the difficult and painful road they traveled as they made an adoption plan for their beloved child. They shared their grief after placement.

They also talked about family and community attitudes toward adoption. Several stressed the need for education regarding adoption, education to help people understand the love and the pain that goes into an adoption decision.

Birthparents' Role in Adoption

The majority of those interviewed played a major role in selecting the adoptive family for their child. They read resumes, they interviewed potential adoptive parents. After choosing the parents, some developed close relationships with the adoptive-parents-to-be. This was more likely to happen, however, in the more recent adoptions. Even five years ago, some spoke of not being allowed to meet the adoptive parents they selected.

These birthparents were quite clear about their unwillingness to turn their newborn (or older child) over to strangers. Many, especially those in more recent adoptions, have no intention of stepping out of their birthchild's life. Nor are the adoptive parents, in many cases, willing to have the birthparents disappear as they were expected to do in the closed, confidential adoptions of yesteryear.

Generally, both the adoptive parents and the birthparents interviewed know their child is likely to feel more secure knowing that both sets of parents love him and care about his welfare. As an adoptive mother said, "No child can get too much love."

Value of Open Adoption

Closed adoption still exists in many parts of the United States and Canada. Some agencies and attorneys don't understand the benefits of open, fully-disclosed adoption *to the child*. This book focuses on counselors/facilitators and clients who shy away from secrets, who know human relationships are likely to go better when based on honesty, not secrets.

Does taking the secretiveness away make a difference? Many people advocating open, fully disclosed adoption think so. Birth and adoptive parents, as they develop strong, extended family relationships for the sake of the child, *know* so.

Pregnant? Adoption Is an Option is especially for pregnant women and couples who might consider an adoption plan *now*. Very little is written here about the absorbing topic of search and reunion in adoption because, with open adoption, there need be no search. The birthparent is already known.

Extended families are not always compatible. It follows that some adoptive and birthfamilies will not be entirely comfortable with each other. For the sake of the child, these birth and adoptive family members need to respect each other and work through their differences if at all possible.

The Open Adoption Experience by Sharon Kaplan Roszia and Lois Molina (1993: Harper Perennial) provides guidelines for planning and carrying out fully open adoptions. Underlying assumption of this book, too, is that openness in adoption is important for the sake of the child. Roszia and Molina discuss ways to develop a good relationship and provide tips for dealing with a relationship that does not go well.

As more and more people hear about the positive choices in truly open adoption, perhaps the next sensationalized story in the media of a "failed" adoption will become simply a tragedy for the individuals involved, rather than having the aura of representing "what is" in adoption. The reality of building open, caring relationships between birth and adoptive families is a world away from these sensationalized stories.

CHAPTER 1

Will You Parent Now?
Or Later?

It was a big shock. I never thought it would happen to me. To other people, yes, but never in a million years would it happen to me.

I looked at all my options and thought, how am I going to go to school, be a good mother, and work all at the same time? It seemed impossible. I knew if I parented, my child would be pushed around from babysitter to babysitter.

My immediate instinct was to want to parent, but I knew that would not be in my child's best interest. I didn't know that much about adoption, but I opened my mind and listened. My view of adoption was how it was in the old days, completely closed. I figured once I made the adoption plan, that would be it. I'd never see her again.

*When I found out about open adoption and realized I
could have as much or as little contact with my child
and the adoptive family as I wished, it changed
everything.*

Katelynn, 19

*I was so confused and scared that I didn't tell anyone
until three days before my baby was born. It was winter,
I'm tall and overweight, and I wore loose clothes. I also
sucked in my stomach a lot. It wasn't real hard to keep it
a secret.*

*I decided on adoption early in my pregnancy. I have
always worked with kids. I teach in a preschool, and
I've cared for children overnight and on weekends. I
knew parenting was a full-time job, and that this baby
was a gift I could give a set of parents.*

Heather, 29

*One of my mom's friends had adopted a little boy
because she couldn't have children. He was a happy
little boy, and the more I thought about it, the more I
realized I'd probably be happier knowing my baby was
alive than if I had an abortion.*

Carmen, 15

Choosing Parenting *or* Adoption

How would you feel if you were a pregnant teenager? Or if
your girlfriend were pregnant? Or you were an older woman
facing an unplanned pregnancy alone? Or a couple who knew
they could not support another child?

Or . . . if you are pregnant now, how do you really feel
about parenting a child? Do you think you have a choice *now*
between being or not being a mother? (Or a father?)

Do you think any discussion of whether or not to parent a
child concerns you? Do you still have options?

Perhaps your friends and/or your parents—and you—

simply assume that because you're pregnant, you're going to
have a baby to raise.

Parenting a child can be one of life's most rewarding tasks.
To parent successfully includes providing not only lots of
love, but also careful guidance, a good environment in which
to grow, and adequate physical, emotional, mental, and
psychological support. This is undoubtedly the greatest
challenge most of us will ever face.

Parenting Your Unborn Child

If you are already pregnant and you've decided to deliver
your baby, you've already made the decision to be a parent.
You are already parenting your unborn child as you provide a
healthy environment for him during those first nine months.
You are parenting well when you eat the foods you and your
baby need during this all-important stage of her life. You are
also parenting well when you keep your prenatal care appointments with your doctor, and when you avoid alcohol, tobacco,
and drugs. You are actively parenting your child from the
moment of conception until he is born.

If you are a man whose partner is pregnant, you, too, are
already parenting. You can support your partner in her efforts
to develop a healthy baby. Together you can plan for your
coming child.

After delivery, you have a choice. You will always be a
parent because you will have a child. Whether you parent
your child yourself or choose another family, through adoption, to be the active parent is your choice. If you choose
adoption, you become a birthparent.

It's a choice you may want to consider.

*As I got bigger, I thought a lot about wanting to keep
my baby. My mother had died the year before, and I
asked my dad if he would help me, and he said he
wouldn't. He said I wasn't ready to be a parent, and he*

was right. I looked at welfare, but there was no way I
wanted to live like that or have my child survive in that
fashion.

Maya

Whether you are a young teenager, a college student, or well-started in your career, this may not be the best time for you to parent.

Many of the babies placed for adoption are first-born children. Their birthparents may intend to be active parents at a later date when they feel they'll be able to parent well.

Others who already have one or more children choose an adoption plan for their new baby. They feel they simply cannot provide for another child at this time.

We may assume that most parents who make an adoption plan are not married. However, people can be married and not feel ready to parent. Or they can be married and choose not to parent, ever. In either case, an adoption plan may be their choice.

Reasons Couples May Plan Adoption

If the father isn't around, a birthmother may choose adoption for that reason—she wants her child to have a father as well as a mother. She decides to make an adoption plan with an adoptive couple.

You might wonder why a couple who care about each other would make an adoption plan. The answer—for some of the same reasons a woman alone plans an adoption. They don't feel they're ready to parent or they don't have the resources to parent at this time.

David, now 28, and Rita, now 23, have been married two years. They placed their baby for adoption almost six years ago. David commented:

We talked a lot all during the pregnancy. From the
fourth to the eight month, we thought of how little we

*really knew each other at that time, and of what comes
out of broken homes, the struggles that single parents
face.*

*Rita had gone through her parents' divorce ten years
earlier. Why do people get divorced? They make quick
decisions, do things they regret later. I didn't want that,
and neither did Rita. We wanted the best for our child.*

*At first we didn't consider adoption because we didn't
know anything about it. Nobody around us seemed to
think about it either. So we went to the Yellow Pages to
find an agency.*

*I think birthfathers need to be honest with themselves.
I had to get rid of that macho idea that I could do
everything. I had to lay aside the things you're "supposed" to be, and get down to reality. That didn't
include parenting at that time.*

Because of their values, David and Rita didn't consider
abortion. Rita remembers the day they first considered
adoption as a possibility:

*One day David and I were in the car driving home
and we looked at each other and said, "What are we
doing?" We hadn't really talked about this, we simply
assumed that if we didn't have an abortion, we would
have a baby. I didn't know anything about adoption. We
went home and sat out on the porch and talked for two
hours. "What are we going to do?"*

*I told him I'm best friends with my mother, we have a
great relationship, but I've seen her go through two
marriages, each going sour, and I knew I wouldn't do
that. If I'm going to have a kid I want a lasting relationship forever, but at 18, only knowing him for three
months, that's not likely. So David said maybe we should
look at adoption. We looked in the phone book and
called an agency.*

The counselor came out to meet with us the first time. Then we made another appointment. I was just two or three weeks away from delivery. I hadn't thought about adoption before. The denial part of it, then the month it took me to tell David, then a month to tell our parents, then seeing the doctors, and the time went so fast I didn't really think about this.

I didn't think about my future, I didn't think about marriage to David, I just thought I was having a baby. I think my mother tried to tell us adoption was an option, but she didn't pressure us either way. Then when we started telling people, everyone was against it. They all said, "You guys can do it. You can make it work. Don't give your baby away."

I think a lot of people look at adoption as the easy way out. Adoption—I think I felt a little bit guilty, that if I do give this baby away, I can still have a life, I can go to college. (She's crying as she talks.) But the decision to do it was to give this baby a real life with two parents to raise it.

David talked about their decision and reasons other people might consider adoption:

Neither of us had really thought about a long-term relationship. We were dating, but neither of us was willing to be married at that point. We weren't that far along in our relationship.

We asked ourselves a lot of questions. Would we be keeping our child just to make ourselves feel good? Would we be able to provide for our child? If we had gotten married and raised this child — what if in a few months we decided we didn't much like each other? Now we're talking about a custody situation, of a child having two separate loyalties.

One of my best friends suffers guilt because if he's

with one divorced parent, he isn't with the other one.

If you're not 100 percent sure you can provide financially, emotionally, and spiritually, you're facing problems. A life is not something you gamble with. I wasn't sure we would ever get to the point of even talking marriage.

The stress and the burden of knowing each other for six months, getting married, having a child . . . Being married is not easy. You have a new relationship with your spouse at the same time you have a new relationship with your child, and there's no balance there.

I wouldn't change anything that has happened. Our son is happy and he has what he deserves, two parents who are crazy about him and who love each other. I don't know how anybody could ever say that was a poor decision.

Adoption Planned for Third Child

Some children placed for adoption have older brothers and sisters. Sometimes a parent realizes that having another baby to support would mean neglecting the child(ren) she already has. Hard as she knows it will be, she may decide to make an adoption plan for the new baby. Aryanna was divorced and already had two children when she got pregnant at 27.

I'm completely alone with my children. I have no child support and my family lives 2000 miles away. The day I found out I was pregnant, there was no question what I was going to do.

I had made a vow that I would not have more children until I was married. I wanted a relationship that would last, and I wanted to have money in the bank, because it's so hard for me and my two boys to survive. They are angels, and thank God we're healthy, but there are a lot of things they don't have. We have struggled so much financially.

Today birthparents in many areas of the United States and Canada can choose the adoptive family for their baby. No longer do they have to "give the baby away" and never see their child again if they make an adoption plan. For some, like Aryanna, this kind of open adoption makes an adoption decision more possible.

Making the Decision

Abortion has been a legal choice for pregnant women in the United States since 1972. Many women with an unplanned pregnancy, however, choose *not* to have an abortion. They choose to continue their pregnancy.

So how do women and their partners make the heavy decision of whether to raise their babies themselves or place them for adoption? Is it usually an emotional decision—"I'd *never* give my baby up for adoption"?

Or, as Diana, 17, put it, "I knew right away I would keep it. It's part of me. At first I thought I could release him for adoption, but then I thought I couldn't stand knowing I have a baby out there somewhere."

These are emotional decisions, but they show the extreme importance of the mother's feelings. Of course these feelings must be seriously considered. Good parenting, however, includes more than feelings. Diana realized rather quickly that she wasn't ready to parent after all. But by the time she came to this conclusion, she didn't feel she had a chance to consider adoption:

> When I was pregnant, I thought my relationship with Chuck would last. I didn't think about adoption until Tina was about five months old. I wanted to (consider adoption) really bad by then, but I didn't have anybody to talk to about it. I didn't know what to do.
>
> A baby needs parents that are a little older and ready to settle down. They can do more things with her and spend more time with her. Now, me, I still want to go out.

There is so much out there that I want to do and see.

I tried to talk to my mom, but she said, "How could you do that?" She is so afraid of what people might think. But I think it would be better for Tina to have two parents.

Pati, too, planned to keep her baby:

I moved back home, and my mom was getting used to the idea that I would keep the baby. Then I went to the agency and decided I'd look at the profiles of the different families. It was the most incredible feeling there. I knew my baby would go to an amazing family. I picked the parents right then and there.

I never felt better in my life. I knew I made the best decision for me. I can go on with my life, finish school, do those things I always wanted to do. My baby will have a mother and father who will love her and give her everything she needs, and I can't.

Loving your baby is crucial, perhaps the most crucial aspect of parenting. But having enough money to feed him/her, living in a place you consider okay for both of you, being able to provide medical care for you and your baby — these unexciting things are also important.

There are other questions to consider. Do you think it's preferable for a child to have a father as well as a mother?

I was adopted when my birthmom was 17. I didn't worry about how my child would feel about me if I placed because I always had the greatest respect for this person who gave me my family. I figured my child would feel the same about me.

They asked me to write a letter to my child. Basically I said if I could live on love alone, that would be fine, but I wanted her to have two parents. I wanted her to be financially stable.

*People still say, "You guys could have gotten by." I
respond, "What is the definition of making do?" I didn't
want to spend my life bitter and angry, and have my
child bitter with me. There are children all over with
bonding disorders because they were passed from
person to person, and they don't have a mom who can
spend enough time with them.*

Lisette

What about *you*? Can you continue your education and/or
career if you're responsible for a child at this time? Can you
prepare for or keep the kind of job you want?

Are you willing to give up a great deal of time to care for
your child? Are you planning how you can take most of this
responsibility, or are you expecting someone else to do much
of the work?

Surely most people don't think having a baby is punish-
ment. However, it is sometimes suggested that if a woman
gets pregnant at the wrong time, she should pay for her
"wrongdoing" by raising the baby.

A student once said, "I will never give my baby up for
adoption. I made a mistake and I'm going to live with my
mistake." One wonders who is being punished—mother
or child.

Family Opposes Adoption Plan

Jazmin, who placed seven years ago, is Hispanic. She faced
strong opposition from her family when she made an adoption
plan. The baby's father had placed his first child for adoption
a year earlier, and he, too, was opposed to Jazmin's
consideration of this option.

Jazmin, who was working and living in her own place,
said:

*I was just getting out on my own. I didn't know
anything about raising kids. I didn't choose to abort the*

baby because I had been through that process before. I called my parents and they said I was on my own.

Then I called the father. We had had a good relationship, but I rarely saw him because he went to school in another city. When I called him, he said he didn't want anything to do with the pregnancy either.

I didn't know what to do when a friend told me about adoption. She gave me a number to call in a city about two hours away. I called Janet, and she was very accepting and warm, so I said I would give it a try.

I packed my stuff a week later, got a job transfer, and moved in May. My baby was born in October seven years ago. During all that time I had no contact with my family.

It worked for me because I made my own decision, I had good counseling from people who cared, and I had positive contact with the adoptive family.

Jazmin feels secure about her adoption decision in spite of her family's opposition. She suggests that each person needs to make her own decision without being influenced by family or friends:

You have to get with what you feel inside. If you let anyone intimidate you or tell you this is wrong, you have to deal with it. I have friends whose family said they shouldn't place and they didn't, and they have bad situations. I have other friends who placed because their families said they had to, and they have to deal with a lot of depression.

You have to search within yourself. You have to think about yourself and you have to think about your child. Sometimes you have to block out what everybody says.

Even today I have friends who look at her pictures and say, "Who is this?" I tell them, and they say, "How could you do that?" My boyfriend doesn't like it and he won't talk about it.

*Everybody has a right to their own opinion, but I'm
not going to get depressed because my boyfriend doesn't
accept it, or my family won't accept it. I'm happy. She's
happy.*

*I know I'll see her sometime. I'm not going to sit
around and be depressed and listen to other people's
comments.*

Analyze Your Choices

If you're pregnant, or your partner is, think about the good
and the not-so-good things about parenthood. To help your
thinking, write down the positive and the negative things
about each possible choice. Each pregnant woman or couple
who has decided against abortion still has at least two
choices—parenting the baby versus placing him for adoption.
Some pregnant women also can choose between staying
single and getting married.

Mark two columns on a sheet of paper. Now write down all
the good things about raising a child—whether you're single
or are/might be married. In another column write down the
good things about *not* having a baby to care for at this point in
your life.

On a second sheet of paper, jot down the things you don't
like about each of your possible choices.

Now, which choice seems to have more positive things
going for you?

While you or your partner is pregnant, you can't make a
legally binding decision to release your baby for adoption. In
most states you must wait until after delivery to sign relinquishment papers. But it's important to consider all your
options long before that time. It's important to make a plan,
whether it's an adoption or a parenting plan.

*Look at all your options. Then make a decision that,
first, is best for your child, and second, is best for you.*

It's important to talk to people who have made different decisions, people who have parented and people who have placed for adoption. Get a view of the whole picture and figure out what's best for your child and what's best for you.

Sometimes parenting is portrayed as this happy existence with this always-happy little baby. You get the baby home and it's a big shock.

Love doesn't buy diapers and food and toys and everything else a baby needs.

Katelynn

Even if you're pregnant now, or your partner is pregnant, you have a choice. You don't need to parent until *you* feel you're ready. Adoption *is* an option.

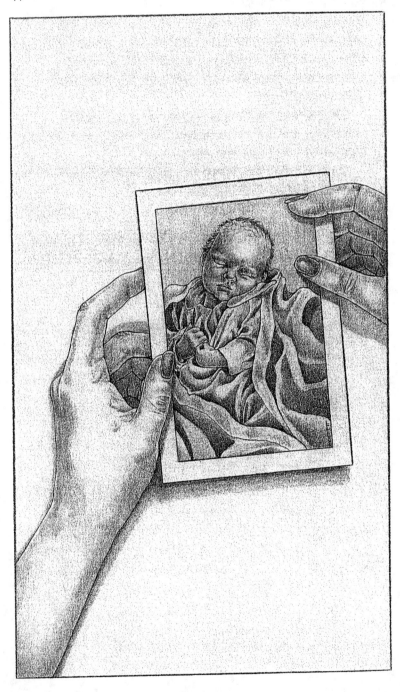

CHAPTER 2

The Changing World of Adoption

After he was born, I languished a lot. I was at home and I felt extremely sorry for myself. I was very depressed and it was hard. My father encouraged me to go to college, and I did go back to school six months later. After that the placement got more and more behind me although not a day went by that I didn't think of him.

I had no support after I placed him. I continued to have some problems, some self-pity. Then I got some counseling, but never any closure. I just went on with my life, always curious about him.

My family, especially my father, had an attitude of "Put it behind you. You'll have other kids." I think it might have helped if I had explored my feelings, had some closure instead of denying it, pushing it away.

Maya—placed baby in closed adoption 14 years ago

*I placed before open adoption was an option. They
didn't allow us to pick a family. I was asking Carolyn
questions, and I got to speak to the lady who handled the
after-care in the foster home.*

*I felt I needed to know more about what actually
happened because I had heard so many horror stories
that I was afraid. I figured I had to get the facts so I
bugged everyone in the front office all through the last
four months of pregnancy.*

Tatum

Closed Adoption No Longer the Rule

Adoption practice is changing rapidly. The drama of one
family rearing the child born to another family remains, but
the details of the script become more and more in tune with
life as many of us know it.

For nearly a century, the fact of a child's adoption was
often hidden from friends and neighbors, perhaps even from
the child himself. The idea was to act as if the child had been
born to the adoptive parents. This was supposed to be the key
to being a "normal" family.

This practice left little room in the adoption picture for the
birthparents. If adoption was "the same as" biological birth,
then the birthparents need not exist. The result tended to be an
adoptive family—adoptee and adoptive parents—together.
The birthparents lurked somewhere in the shadows.

This seemed to work for several generations. Unmarried
pregnancy was considered a sin that needed to be kept hidden
from the child. The less the adoptive parents knew about their
child's birthparents, the less they would have to tell their child
about them. And if they knew nothing about the birthparents,
they *couldn't* talk about them. Closed (confidential) adoption
became the norm. As soon as the child was born, the
birthparents were to disappear.

It wasn't always like this. The first closed adoption (sealed records) law was passed in Minnesota in 1917. Within 30 years, closed adoption laws had been passed all across the United States. Some of those laws remain in effect today.

These laws meant that secrecy was big in adoption. Birthparents were not told where their children were. They were not told much about the families rearing their children. As the years passed, they knew nothing about their child's life, indeed, whether their child was even alive.

Adoptees, of course, faced the same secrecy. Generally they knew nothing about their birthparents. They did not know *why* these birthparents elected to have someone else take over the parenting of their child. From lack of knowledge, it was easy for adoptees to assume they were throwaway babies, children whose birthparents did not love them. Otherwise, why were they not with these birthparents?

In confidential adoption, the answers were missing.

For some adoptees, it didn't seem to be a big deal. Their lives were good, they loved their families. There didn't seem to be a need to know about their birthparents, or, if there was, that need was kept carefully hidden.

Adoptees Search for Birthparents

Other adoptees felt strongly about the missing links in their lives. So strongly, in fact, that many searched for their birthparents. Sometimes those searches resulted in reunions between adoptee and birthparents.

> *I found out I was adopted when I was in kindergarten. Somebody there used the word "adoption" and I didn't know what it meant. I went home and asked my mother, and she told me.*
>
> *She also said I was adopted. I said, "Oh, okay," because when you're five, you don't really care as long as dinner is on the table.*
>
> *When I was ten it started to bother me. I started having all these feelings about who I was and where I*

*was going. I didn't look like my parents or my sister, and
I was curious to see if I might look like my birthfamily.*

*When I was 16, I called a few places but they said I
couldn't do anything about finding my birthparents until
I was 18. Soon after my 18th birthday my adoptive
parents called the adoption agency where they got me.
The counselor there gave us some information but she
couldn't give me my birthparents' last names.*

*I did some detective work on my own—managed to
check my hospital birth records and learned my
birthmother's name.*

*I was born in a suburb of Los Angeles and had been
told she was a college student. I figured if she couldn't
afford to keep me, she must have been attending a
community college. She probably couldn't afford UCLA
or USC.*

*I went to the library of the city college near her
childhood home, asked for the 1966 yearbook. And there
it was, my birthmother's picture. I couldn't believe how
much she looked like me. Believe me, I was excited!*

*Then my dad helped me contact a search group. I
talked to a woman there, and she asked me a lot of
questions.*

"What if you find she's dead?"

"What if she denies she's your mother?"

"What if you don't like her?"

*I told her I wanted to find her and my birthfather, that
I felt I was prepared for whatever might happen. By then
I knew my birthfather's name.*

*She called me a few hours later. She said she had
found my mother's marriage record and had her current
address. She was living only 40 miles away. I called
information and got her phone number.*

*At the time I was seeing a counselor, and I asked him
to contact her for me. He called her and said, "I have*

someone in my office who has reason to believe she is your daughter."

She was startled to say the least, and she told the counselor she wanted to talk with him first.

He called me the next day and asked me to come over. She was in his office. I said "Hi," and she said, "Don't I get a hug after all these years?"

Then she started crying, and I said, "Don't do that."

I've seen her nearly every week since then, and we talk on the phone. We have a good relationship.

My grandpa kicked her out of the house when she was pregnant, and she couldn't afford to keep me. She fed me and spent time with me while she was in the hospital.

I found my birthfather a couple of months later. I look exactly like him. He had never known my mom was pregnant because he'd gone overseas right after she conceived.

His mother, my grandma, was all excited at having another grandchild. She told all their relatives back east, and she keeps talking about how much we look alike.

Kellie, 19 — an adoptee

If Kellie's birthparents and adoptive parents could have arranged the kind of open adoption available today, her search would not have been necessary.

Not all reunions are as satisfying as Kellie's. Occasionally, a birthparent did not want to be found, or perhaps the birthparent and the adoptee did not have much in common after their years apart. However, the reunion provided answers about their lost birth heritage. "I finally understand who I am," an adoptee commented.

Adoptive parents sometimes were afraid the reunion would mean losing the child they had reared and loved. If their child found her "real" parents, her birthparents, would they lose this son or daughter? This seldom happened. To the adoptee, the adoptive parents were the "real" parents, the parents who reared him. The need to find his birthparents did not damage his tie with his other parents.

Birthparents Didn't Forget

During those years of secret adoptions, the birthparents in the shadows were expected to "give up" their baby and return to life as they knew it. They were supposed to forget the birth had ever occurred. In this way, their lives could go on, undisrupted by this poorly timed pregnancy.

The reality, of course, was far different. Birthparents' lives were changed forever. They never forgot the child they had released. Many had a difficult time working through the grief they felt but were not supposed to acknowledge.

I was 16, a senior in high school, raised in a strict Catholic family. My mom and dad were separated and getting a divorce, lots of bitterness. I knew I was pregnant three or four months before anyone else knew except I told the father right away. We thought we were in love and would live happily ever after. He was 16, too.

When my mom found out I was pregnant, she went off the deep end and she sent me to a maternity home. I was supposed to be due late January. I went into the home late in October and delivered in December. I wanted to keep the baby but I had no rights.

I assumed that the birthfather, since he was on the outside, could do something to fight for our rights but that never happened. After I came home we never spoke about it. It was a done deal. I was to put it behind me.

Everyone in school believed I was staying with my grandma, and I left it at that. I never discussed it with anyone. I met my husband the following August, my knight in shining armor. He was there to pick up the pieces. I told him about the adoption the first night.

We married, and we have three daughters. I told him that one day I would search for my son because it was very important to me to explain to him why he was placed for adoption.

I kept my son with me a couple of days while I was in the hospital even though I wasn't supposed to. The husband of a woman there took a picture for me. I told him my baby had jaundice and was staying behind. I still have that picture today.

My mom didn't even want me to see the baby or know anything about him. I tried hard to parent while I was pregnant—music, talking to him. I did everything I could to parent well.

I was supposed to totally forget it. I was never supposed to mention the baby, the father, the experience. I was a good girl and I did exactly what my mom told me to do. No one ever brought it up—three brothers, one sister, and no mention of that baby ever again except to my husband.

I went back to school and played the game of going to my grandma's house and taking care of her. I graduated.

I used to have nightmares, bad dreams, and I went to counseling off and on. It has ruined my life in lots of ways. It has left some deep scars, a lot of anger.

I have basically forgiven my mom for what she did.

Veronica — placed baby 17 years ago, closed adoption

Birthmom Reunites with Son

Many birthparents decided to search for their relinquished children. They had an extremely strong need to know if these children were alive, if they were well and happy. Veronica described her search and reunion with her son:

I started searching two years ago. I went back to the Catholic Social Service, and ended up with the same

*worker I had had earlier. She always felt she was there
for me, but I don't think anyone was there for me. They
were there for my mom. Nobody ever said to me, "If you
want to keep this baby we can offer you a medical
card . . ." Nobody ever thought of me as a possible
parent.*

*I asked her if she would contact Jim. I knew she knew
where he was. They also named him Jim, as I had done.*

*I didn't even let anyone in my family know I was
trying to find him because I was afraid somebody would
try to intervene. I had written back and forth to the
adoptive family several times before I told my family.
Then I called a family meeting and told them what I was
going to do.*

*One brother thought it was okay, but the rest thought
I should let bygones be bygones.*

*It was hard to sit down with them and tell them I had
made contact with Jim. I think I was afraid of losing
them, or of them interfering with my relationship with
him. Everybody dearly loves him now.*

We're only a year into it. It's working very well.

*I never wanted to place my child for adoption to
begin with. When I left the hospital I went to the nursery
and told Jim that some day I would find him and explain
to him why this happened. Nobody was going to keep me
from that.*

*I believe that adoption should be open, not just one
letter a year or a picture, but ongoing communication. I
don't want the child confused, but as much involvement
as possible with the adoptive family and the birthfamily
together can only enhance a child's life. Nobody ever
has too many people loving them.*

For a more detailed account of birthmothers during the era
of closed adoption, see *Birthmothers* by Merry Bloch Jones
(1993: Chicago Review Press).

Adoption Rate Goes Down

When the Sexual Revolution came along in the 60s and 70s, unmarried pregnancy was no longer considered a disgrace to be hidden at all costs. No longer was it assumed that a single woman could not parent a child alone.

With these changes, a downward spiral in adoptive placements began. In the 1950s, the majority of single pregnant teens, as many as 85 percent, placed their babies for adoption. By the mid 80s, less than four percent did so.

Secrecy is not considered a healthy practice in other areas of human relationships. Yet secrecy was still the rule in adoption. And it wasn't healthy for most people involved in the adoption triangle.

Infant adoption became rare. Secrecy in adoption simply didn't fit any longer. The culture had changed.

Slowly, slowly adoption began to change. First, birthmothers were encouraged to write letters to their infants, letters which the adoptive parents would share with the child at a later date. In these letters, the child was assured he was not a cast-off, unwanted baby.

Birthparents described how much they loved this baby after bonding throughout the nine months of pregnancy. They explained they were making an adoption plan so that this beloved child would have a better chance in life than they could provide at that time.

Before long, some adoptive parents began writing letters back to the birthparents. This evolved, in some instances, into continuing correspondence, sometimes including the exchange of photos.

Gradually, contact between birth and adoptive parents became more and more commonplace, with actual meetings being set up by some agencies and independent adoption services.

Always, there was concern for the child. Change is difficult for some people, and openness progressed very slowly in some areas, more rapidly in others. Janet Fish, Marywood Children and Family Services, Austin, Texas, commented:

> *This is our 75th year of operation at Marywood. The caring and the nurturing of birthparents has not changed over the years but the openness is a drastic change. We have several levels of openness depending upon the comfort level of the parties involved. We do our best to honor the birthparents' requests.*
>
> *We share profiles of adoptive parents who most closely meet the birthparents' wishes, and they generally meet face-to-face before the child is born. Once the child is placed, the adoptive parents and birthparents may share photos, letters, and gifts through the agency. If both parties decide to fully disclose and share directly, they are able to do so. Some do, but not as many as one might expect.*
>
> *We accept families into our program who are open to meeting birthparents and continuing correspondence since almost all of our birthparents are wanting that level of openness. Most adoptive couples understand the importance of this process, particularly after they have had a face-to-face meeting. I believe this is so valuable because they connect with the birthparents at that time, and are then able to convey a three-dimensional picture of them to the adoptee as she or he grows. The bonding that takes place during the meeting is important to the future relationship of everyone involved in the adoption.*

Open Adoption Works

Open adoption pioneers often pointed out that in most of the world during most of known history, some children have been raised by families other than their birthfamilies, and these "adoptions" seldom were or are secret. If open adoption worked in other areas of the world, why wouldn't it work here?

Why indeed? We have learned from observing open adoptions through the years, that it does work, apparently much better than secrecy worked.

As you consider an adoption plan versus a parenting plan, know that you can and should be in charge of planning your baby's future. If active parenting is your choice, you know you need to figure where you and your child will live. You need to think about financial security for your child. The list goes on and on. As your child's parent, you know it is your responsibility to make these plans.

If adoption is your choice, you have similar responsibilities. You still need to make a plan, only now you will choose another family to nurture your child, care for him in the way you want him cared for.

A generation ago, you would have had to trust the adoption agency or your attorney or other adoption facilitator to choose that family. Now you can make responsible decisions yourself for your child's welfare. And who is better equipped to do so than you—your child's first parent?

This is not to imply that carrying out an adoption plan will be easy. Very little about adoption—or parenting—is easy. With counseling and family support, however, it can work.

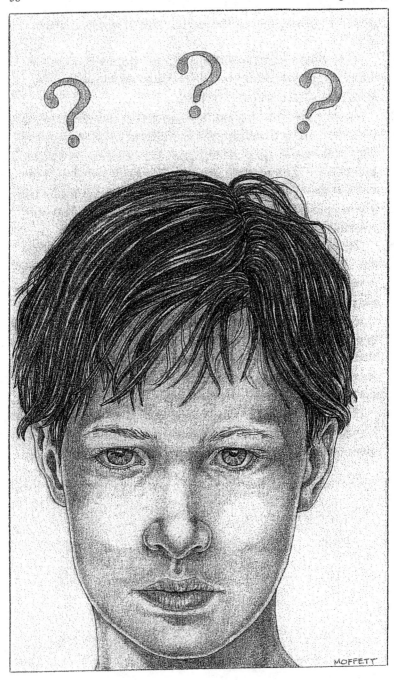

CHAPTER 3

To Be or Not to Be — A Teenage Parent

I was about 14 when I found I was pregnant. The scariest part was telling my mom. I was growing up in one of those families that if you ever get pregnant, you pack your bags and go. I knew I was pregnant because I hadn't had a period.

I waited until 3 A.M., I packed my clothes, cleaned out my dresser drawers, and put my bags by the front door. I woke my mom up and said, "I'm pregnant."

She was sleeping, and she sat up and said "What?" And I jumped off the bed.

"What are you going to do?" she asked.

I started crying and said, "I don't know."

I told her I thought my only option was abortion. I made an appointment and she was to go with me, but that morning she told me she really didn't want me to do that. She said there were other options.

The agency we called first said they would not accept interracial babies, so we went down to Marywood and did the entrance interview. I wasn't sure adoption was what I wanted to do. I went back and forth between deciding whether to keep the baby or place the baby throughout the whole pregnancy. One day, "I'm going to keep," the next day, "I'm going to place." The more I learned about adoption, the less afraid of it I became.

Tatum

I was 14 when I got pregnant. I wasn't expecting it because we used birth control, but the condom broke. I figured right away that I was pregnant.

I didn't have to tell my parents. My dad knew, and my mom found out from one of her friends. She was mad at me, and she wanted me to have an abortion.

My boyfriend and I weren't ever really together. He told me he didn't want to have anything to do with the baby. We talked while I was pregnant, but we weren't together. He said he would pay for an abortion, but I didn't want that. "What are you going to do?" he asked.

I told him I was considering adoption. He never really decided anything. He just went along with whatever I decided.

Carmen

Why Don't More Teens Make Adoption Plans?

A couple of generations ago, many pregnant teenagers relinquished (gave up, released, surrendered) their babies for adoption. An unmarried adolescent who became pregnant was often hustled off to Aunt Agatha's home in Missouri where she lived until her baby was born.

Usually the young mother didn't see her baby at all. It was placed for adoption with a family she would never meet, and the entire event was wrapped in secrecy. Her friends were told she was vacationing with Aunt Agatha, and she was urged to forget the whole episode and return to "normal" life as a teen.

This picture changed twenty or thirty years ago. Women of all ages in the United States have a legal right to an abortion during the early months of pregnancy (although in some states, women younger than 18 must have either their parent's permission or the court's approval). Each year about one-third of the million teenage pregnancies end in induced abortion. Another one out of six ends in spontaneous miscarriage.

Very few teens make adoption plans for their babies, less than four percent of the half-million who give birth each year in the United States. There are several reasons that so few pregnant adolescents consider adoption.

First and most important, they, like all pregnant women, bond with their babies before birth. They love their babies just as older mothers do, and adoption is an extremely hard and painful decision to make.

Second, the younger an adolescent is, the less likely she is to make an adoption plan. Developmentally, people in early adolescence find it difficult to look ahead. Getting through the pregnancy may be all she can handle. Trying to figure out what's best for her child and herself for the next 18 years may be almost impossible. Making any kind of plan may require more maturity than she has had a chance to develop.

If you're a teenager, the fact that you're reading this book probably means you're more mature than many other pregnant teens. You *are* concerned about the future—but that doesn't make your decision easy.

Many pregnant teens do not know how much adoption has changed in the past decade. If you think that adoption means giving your baby away to strangers, and you assume you would never see your child again, adoption may seem impossible.

Teens who are more interested in the adoption option are likely to be those who plan an open adoption. They choose the adoptive parents for their child, and they plan to stay in contact with their child.

You'll Get Lots of Advice

If you're a teenager and you're pregnant, you're probably getting lots of advice. Some people feel teens are not mature enough to make big decisions about a baby.

You'll undoubtedly hear, "What do you mean, you'll *keep* that baby? You aren't old enough to be a parent." These people assume that "of course" you'll make an adoption plan.

Probably an adoption plan has *not* been made by a number of young women and their partners because of comments like this. "We'll show them" is sometimes the reaction—along with the feeling that, *at the time*, keeping your baby to rear yourself may be an easier decision to make.

On the other hand, you're probably surrounded by people who can't believe you'd "give your baby away." Your peers who aren't pregnant and who don't have children may remind you that your baby "will be so cute." They may assure you that they'll help with babysitting. "Of course you can manage," they may say.

Some families are convinced that the only responsible answer to too-early pregnancy is adoption. A couple of generations ago, most families felt this way if the young couple was not married. Your family may remind you of the importance of a child having two parents who are married and who live together, parents who can financially support themselves and their child. Your child "should" be with another family who can offer these things, they may say.

Or, and this is the more likely scenario, your family may be appalled at the idea of another family rearing your child. "Not our flesh and blood" is a typical remark.

If a woman is past 20 and living on her own, other people's opinions may add stress to her decision-making efforts. However, she, along with her partner, can usually make her own decision. But if you're a teenager, you may wonder how you'll *ever* make a decision that will please everybody.

The answer, of course, is that you probably can't please

everybody. Your biggest concern is your baby. Your next biggest concern needs to be yourself. Somehow, you have to figure out the best plan for you and your baby, then help your friends, and especially your family, understand. You need their support.

Too much advice can make decision-making very hard. After listening to that advice, you and your partner need to make the best decision you possibly can. If you help your family understand *why* you make that decision, they're more likely to be supportive.

> *The decision-making process was difficult. Nick came to me and said, "I'm not ready to be a father. I think we should look at adoption."*
>
> *I was livid. "How can you say that?" I didn't want to be responsible for any information on adoption because then I'd have to think about it.*
>
> *I was seven months along when, as I was driving home from church, I started crying. I knew I couldn't keep her. It was a fantasy that I could have this baby and the world be the way I wanted it to be. I went home and told my mom, and we both sat at the kitchen table crying.*

> Kathleen

As with the less important decisions you make each day, the more you use good judgment and clear-headed thinking to work out your final adoption or parenting plan, the more your family will concur. Perhaps they will realize you *are* mature enough to do what you've decided is best for you and your baby.

Making the Decision

If most pregnant teenagers *choose* to keep their babies to rear themselves, their decision must be respected. It is possible for a young single mother to do a fine job of parenting, especially if she has a good support system within her family.

But is that choice consciously made? Or is becoming a mother often simply acceptance of what seems to be — that if one is pregnant and doesn't get an abortion, one will usually have a baby (true), and therefore raise that baby oneself (not necessarily true)?

Many young women are "successful" mothers. They give their children the care they need, sometimes at great sacrifice to themselves. They love their children deeply. But it is difficult to know who will be a good parent and who will not, whether that parent is single or married, 15 or 25 years old. Some 25-year-old parents neglect their children. And sometimes a 15-year-old does a beautiful job of mothering.

Nita, 15, and Joe, also 15, were shocked at their positive pregnancy test. They figured they would keep their child, but soon after they took Zach home from the hospital they realized they were not ready to parent. Nita explained:

Joe was in denial for a couple of months. I figured I'd have my baby, I'd raise it, and then I'd have my life. But it didn't work out that way.

After Zach was born, I didn't want to hold him. I loved him, but I didn't have that motherly instinct. I was concerned for him, but I really wanted to be a teenager.

I moved in with Joe and his mother so I could go to a school with childcare. Zach and I went back and forth to school on the city bus, but he kept getting sick.

My grandma had always talked to me about adoption. Then I was talking to a counselor at school about my problems, and she said it wasn't too late for adoption. Zach was two months old then. I mentioned it to Joe, and he said he'd been thinking about it, too, but he didn't say anything because he didn't want to upset me.

We decided to go ahead. We talked to an adoption counselor, and we picked out a couple. Three weeks later Zach was gone.

I didn't have regrets but I was very disappointed in myself. I've been through so much in my life, and I always wanted my child to have a mother and father who would always be there, and who wouldn't ever have money problems.

My mom had me when she was 17, and she's right now still trying to get back her wild years.

My mother was very very sad about the adoption, and she had to go to counseling. My brother and sister took it hard. I'm trying to teach my sister that having a baby may look like fun. It looks easy, but it isn't.

Teens tend to think "My baby will love me. I'll dress him up all cute and everybody will love me." But they aren't looking at the late nights, the crying. They aren't thinking, "How am I going to get to the doctor when I can't even drive yet?" I didn't like relying on other people.

Joe commented:

When I finally realized I would be a father, I was all happy. Nita mentioned adoption back then, but I said, "Let's keep it. We can handle it." So I quit going to school, and I got a job.

It didn't work out. We couldn't afford him, and we weren't even living together after she went back home. She and my mom didn't get along.

I started thinking about adoption after Zach was born. He was more expensive than I thought — the diapers, the formula . . . and sometimes I'd miss out on work because I had to watch him.

We were all sad. When I'm in my room by myself, I think about him. It's getting better as time goes by. We're getting pictures of the baby pretty often.

I want to parent when I can afford it, when I have a place of my own—maybe when I'm 30!

"Nobody Knew"

Often a young woman keeps her pregnancy secret from everyone for several months:

> *Nobody knew for several months except the birthfather. I was 16, and I didn't want to accept reality. Then when I finally accepted it, I didn't want to let anybody know because I had let people down.*
>
> *The birthfather would call and ask what he could do, but I kind of pushed him out, too. I wanted to do this on my own, and I see now that wasn't a good thing.*
>
> *Finally I let my closest aunt know. She said, "Are you sure?"*
>
> *I said, "Yes. I sit in class and feel the baby moving." So she came over and told my parents. That was very emotional, the first time I ever saw my father cry.*
>
> *We found an agency we liked, and that was the best thing that happened. I enrolled there the last 1 1/2 months, and they helped me a lot with information and sorting out my thoughts on what I would do.*
>
> *During all this time I was alone, I thought, "I'm not ready for this. I don't want my child to come into this world and not have what I have."*
>
> *I wanted her to have two parents, and I wanted her to have more than I could give. I didn't have a job, and I didn't want to rob her of anything. So I decided adoption was best.*
>
> Yvette

If you, like Yvette, are not talking to anyone about your pregnancy, that may be the first thing you need to do. You may be afraid to tell your parents, but over and over, my students have told me how their parents, after an initial outburst, quickly became supportive of their pregnant daughter. Your family may be more supportive than you expect.

Sonia, like so many teens, had a hard time telling her

parents she was pregnant. When she finally did, their support became an important part of her decision-making:

I was 16, a junior in high school, and Jake and I had been together about six months. I knew I was pregnant that first month. I went into denial—I didn't tell anybody, not even Jake. I was on the track team, running five miles a day cross-country.

I knew my being pregnant would hurt my parents, and I didn't know how to approach them. I was scared, and I withdrew from them and from all my friends. I didn't want to be around anybody. I wore baggy clothes. The first time I felt him move inside me I just wanted to die.

When I finally told Jake I was pregnant, he was as scared as I was.

Then one day I woke up and realized this baby was important. Somehow I knew it was not for me, but I needed to take care of it. I told my parents, and they were real upset. I had never seen my dad cry before. My brothers were very upset, too.

After a few days they came around with "We're going to support you in whatever you decide to do." That meant the world to me. I don't think I could have gone through it without my mom.

Placing Joshua was the hardest thing I ever did in my life. It changed my life, turned my life around and made me a better person. If I had it to do over again, I would place him again, even with what I went through with Jake. I live with it every day of my life. Not a day goes by that I don't think of Joshua. His happiness keeps me going.

Talking with Birthmother Helps

Maggie, pregnant at 17, worked part-time in an office with a birthmother who talked about her child's adoption. Otherwise, Maggie might never have considered an adoption plan:

Six years ago I got pregnant, three months before I graduated.

I didn't know anything about adoption—it's not talked about much. But I was lucky to be working with a girl who had gone through an adoption, and I knew about it because she was very open.

If it had not been for her, I might never have thought about adoption.

If you don't know much about adoption, one of the best things you can do is find a birthparent, either an individual or a birthparent support group, and learn about their experiences. Maggie continued:

I always thought I would go to college, get married, then have kids, in that order. And I knew I wasn't emotionally ready to parent.

So after this friend and I talked, I called a counselor at an agency. She explained all about adoption and all the different ways to go about it. That's what I liked, the flexibility where you and the adoptive parents make the decisions.

The father was out of the picture because we had broken up. I did tell him, and at first he was supportive. Then a few days later he came over and told me he didn't want to have any more to do with me, no matter what I wanted to do.

I felt I couldn't give my child either the emotional or financial support I had growing up. This was important to me. I was scared, especially as to what people would think of me. I was afraid people would think I was uncaring, and didn't love my child. But I knew that wasn't so.

I tried not to become attached to my baby while I was pregnant, but of course you do.

I had a good support system with my friends and my mother. It was hard to do, and I can't imagine going through it without support.

How Does Adoption Affect Children?

Do you know adopted children who have known they were adopted, that they are "special," for as long as they can remember? For some birthparents, hearing from adoptees how they feel about adoption helps:

> *They had a program at the maternity home where you could meet people who had adopted. They brought their children to a picnic, and I said I'd babysit. There was a little girl who was three, another seven or eight, and another who was ten, and all three were adopted. They knew much more about adoption than I did.*
>
> *The youngest little girl asked me, "Are you going to have your baby adopted?"*
>
> *I said "What do you know about adoption?"*
>
> *She said, "I'm adopted and I have two sets of parents. My mommy says I'm more loved because I have four parents." Then she said, "Your baby would be so loved" — this from a three-year-old!*
>
> *I also got to meet my counselor's two adopted children, a daughter two years older than me, and a son four years older. I told her they were so like her and she said, "You know they are adopted???" And I was thunderstruck because they seemed so happy.*
>
> *I started thinking more and more about adoption.*
>
> Tatum

Having, caring for, and loving children are joyful situations for many people. It is an especially joyful happening if the timing is "right ." Parenthood at 17—or even 15—may be right for some people. But postponing parenthood for a few years might make it more joyful for others.

Adoption is an option!

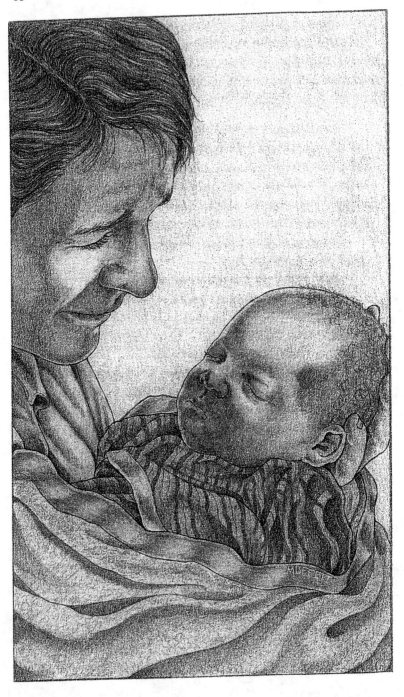

CHAPTER 4

Birthfathers Are Parents Too

We saw the counselor at least 20 times, but I felt left out because she didn't seem to include me particularly. I think she feels if there is a supportive man, why would you place the child for adoption? They have these support groups which seem to help Danielle, but, except for one night when they invited me, it was just the mothers.

I felt like I was the only man in town who, if they weren't married, existed after the conception.

We didn't consider abortion. Parenting might have been exciting, but virtually impossible in a responsible manner. I don't want to go to a store with food stamps just to feed my child. It was the wrong time. You have to get your immediate family in order before you bring more members in.

Danielle is going to one of these group meetings

*tomorrow night. I asked her if I could go, but it's for
women.*

Derek

*In my support group I was the only one whose
birthdad stuck around, and our meetings tended to turn
into a bash-the-man discussion. I think it's real important that people arranging these adoptions realize there
is a man around. Derek went through everything that I
did, at least emotionally, and he didn't get nearly as
much support.*

*Adoption tends to be very much centered on the
female. I don't think our adoption counselor really knew
how to deal with a couple although she did a good job.*

*When I told people I was still with Derek, they would
say, "Well, why are you giving your baby up?"*

*I'd tell them, "Just because you have somebody in
your life doesn't mean this is the time to parent."*

Danielle

Birthfathers Often Ignored

Adoption begins with birthparents, yet they are often
overlooked in discussions of adoptees and their adoptive
families. Even advice columnist Ann Landers tends to put
birthparents in the shadows with her tendency to focus on the
overriding importance of the adoptive parents.

Even when birthparents are brought out of those shadows,
they generally are *birthmothers*. Every adopted child also has
a birthfather somewhere, but that fact is often ignored.

Many birthmothers place their babies for adoption because
the father won't be parenting his child. The mothers want their
children reared in a two-parent family. The birthfather needs
to sign the relinquishment papers to make the adoption legal,
but other than his signature, he is often out of the picture.

Many birthfathers probably would prefer to be included.
Over time in an open adoption, most children would benefit

from having the birthfather involved.

> *Our counselor said Steve was the first birthfather she*
> *had talked with. That was incredible to me.*
>
> *We're still together. When I told him I was pregnant,*
> *he was surprised but not upset. We immediately started*
> *talking about how we'd take care of this baby. He was*
> *working full-time, but we figured he could get a second*
> *job. We talked a lot about marriage, but I thought it was*
> *too early in our relationship to make that commitment.*
>
> *I talked with Janet (adoption counselor) twice by*
> *myself. After that, he went with me. It was hard on me,*
> *but I think I made the adoption decision more easily*
> *than Steve did. I think his problem was that he didn't feel*
> *good enough. We talked so much about how we didn't*
> *have enough money to take care of this baby, and I think*
> *he thought that was his fault.*
>
> *He has the old-fashioned idea that it's the man's job*
> *to take care of the family, and that he was to blame. We*
> *talked a lot. He was my support through the whole thing,*
> *and I think I was his. It was good to have him around.*
>
> Sabrina

Many Birthfathers Do Care

Some men simply don't stick around when they learn their
partner is pregnant. That doesn't mean birthfathers as a group
don't care. Each birthfather is an individual with unique
thoughts and feelings, just as each birthmother is unique. To
generalize that birthfathers don't care is a gross injustice to
those who do. Sometimes he doesn't appear to care because,
for whatever reason, he isn't *allowed* to be involved.

Yvette started considering adoption soon after she admitted
she was pregnant at three months. She thought she might have
a problem with the birthfather:

> *At first he said, "You're going to do this? But we have*
> *a future together. We'll get married and I'll get a job."*

And I would think, "Reality, get ahold of him!"

My mother called him over to my house to tell him my decision, and if he had a problem with it, we needed to work it out.

He said, "No, no problem. Times are hard. We both need to get out of school." He signed the papers.

Nick and Kathleen Plan Together

Nick is 25 now, a junior high science teacher and football coach. He was 18 when Kathleen, a year younger, got pregnant. Both he and Kathleen were very active in school. He was co-captain of the football team, she was a musician, and both were college-bound National Honor Society students.

The pregnancy was a major shock. Kathleen's mother took her to the doctor because she suspected something. Kathleen called me at 3 A.M. and told me. My mother was out of town that weekend and I was alone that night, so I had a lot of time to think.

When my mom came home, I told her. She and my dad were divorced, and he lived out of state.

Kathleen was against abortion, so we assumed we would parent. However, her parents said we couldn't see each other any more, that if they caught us together, Kathleen would be sent off to relatives and I would never see her again. For about two months we communicated only by passing notes at school. Her siblings were there keeping an eye on us. We had to be careful.

I didn't get to wrestle or run track that season. Mentally I couldn't focus because I was too concerned with the situation. I tried to run track but I had started a job on the weekends and there wasn't time to practice.

I agreed to pay half the expenses. Luckily her parents' insurance would pay the medical bills.

Neither of us thought of adoption at first, but her

grandmother brought up the idea. She gave us some books and videos to help us learn about it. We talked about it, and we started going to counseling together. We also went to birthparent support group and pregnant teen meetings. Through all this, we realized adoption was probably the best solution to our problem.

I think I decided on adoption first because I came from a split home and I knew what it was like to be reared by a single parent. I didn't want to go through a divorce and put my child through what I had experienced. That was a major fear for me.

One day we developed a budget. We wrote down what we thought we could provide and what we would need. The best job I ever had paid minimum, $3.25 an hour. We worked out a budget with me working for $5 an hour, and realized I would have to work 50 to 70 hours a week to make ends meet. And that was if I was lucky enough to find a job with benefits.

We were already paying the pregnancy expenses. We paid for our counseling appointments. Kathleen made a lot of her clothes, but we paid for them. I think it was good for us to see those expenses because it helped us realize what it would be like with a baby to support. Up until then, everything had been taken care of by our families.

We also knew Kathleen needed to finish school. My mom already worked two jobs and couldn't babysit. Her parents both worked and were very involved in raising a family of four kids.

We looked at it as if we were going it alone, which was the reality. When I looked at me being the provider, I didn't feel at all comfortable. Even if I could provide financially, I felt I couldn't provide emotionally because I was still a kid. I had no job skills. I played football. There was nothing marketable about me.

*We talked about it a lot and realized everything
wasn't going to be okay. We wanted the best for our
daughter, and also what was best for us. Adoption
seemed the best plan.*

Birthfathers Need Support Too

In spite of Nick's caring concern for Kathleen and their
unborn child, and his willingness to attend counseling and
support groups with Kathleen, he didn't feel his needs were
considered:

*The counselor at the agency said something I have
never forgotten, something that really bothered me. I
was there for Kathleen, I was expected to be there, but
the social worker told me there was nothing they could
do for me. If I wanted to sit in on Kathleen's counseling
sessions, they would allow it, but they didn't have
anything going for males. I felt betrayed.*

*It was a hard time. It was so centered around the
female that the male was forgotten. I was very involved
and felt connected. I cut the cord, and we took care of
our child for three days in the hospital. With all that, I
had a lot of emotional ties.*

In the past, when birthmothers were expected to give birth,
release the baby in a closed adoption, and go home, forgetting
the whole experience, many of those birthmothers faced tough
times. All birthparents grieve, and we know now that after-
placement counseling can be an important part of dealing with
that grief. Nick didn't have that help. His life was to go on as
if the baby had never happened. He continued his story:

*When I went off to college (with a full academic and
football scholarship), my life started falling apart. I quit
going to class. I lost 30 pounds in one month. I didn't
want to get out of bed. I was sick but they couldn't find
anything wrong with me. I realize now I was deeply*

depressed. My relationship with Kathleen had fallen
apart, so I had lost my girlfriend and my daughter.

I had a lot of time there at school, several hours a
day, that I would just think. I dropped out of school
within two months. I didn't get a job, and my family was
very upset with me.

I moved in with my dad and his wife who lived out in
the country. It was very calm, it was wintertime, and I
had a lot of time to sit and think and reflect.

I got a job in a box factory, and soon realized that
wasn't what I wanted to do the rest of my life. I remem-
ber one night looking around as I worked, and I realized
it was over. I would get back to school and try to be a
teacher. That's what I'd always wanted to do. So I went
home, shaved off my beard, and started contacting
colleges. I was back in school by September.

As I look back, I realize the support I received around
the adoption was not enough. I felt it was my duty to be
by Kathleen's side but I wasn't supposed to grieve as she
did because I was the male. Males need support too.

Rachel Waldorf, birthmother and, for several years, counselor with Children's Home Society of Minnesota, stressed that
counselors' attitudes should be the same toward birthfathers as
toward birthmothers. "Sometimes they focus on the birthmother and leave the birthfather out, even if he's sitting right
beside her," she commented. "I remember sitting in counseling with my baby's father, and the counselor would look at me
and talk to me directly. He was left out.

"There are also attorneys who bad-mouth birthfathers
terribly," she added. "You need to find somebody sensitive to
birthfathers as well as birthmoms."

If Birthmother Is Alone

Wendy Heiser, Bethany Christian Services, Seattle, Washington, reports that she works with the birthfather when she

can. "I surely encourage it," she said, "but about 98 percent of the time he isn't around. I think he's often scared. He can't afford to parent. It's too bad, because I see it as a time for these men to grow, but a lot of them don't stick around.

"We have our adoptive families write "Dear Birthfather" along with their "Dear Birthmother" letters. We encourage him to be supportive for the sake of his child. It's a matter of trying to help them look beyond 'This is my blood' to 'What is best for my child?'"

> *I think he was really scared, and he didn't know how to react. He was only 18, a year younger than I was, and his parents gave him a hard time about the pregnancy.*
>
> *Not long before I delivered I reconciled with him because I want him to be available if our daughter ever wants to meet him. He came to see me in the hospital, and I send him pictures when I get them.*
>
> Katelynn

Deane Borgeson of The Adoption Connection, Highland Park, Illinois, reports that about 30 percent of their birthmother clients are involved with the birthfathers. These birthfathers tend to be involved in the adoption process. "Birthmothers really need to understand that for the sake of the baby they should name the birthfather. Otherwise the birthfather can contest an adoption with little effort," Borgeson said.

You may agree that birthfathers *should* be involved, but the birthfather of your baby may even refuse to acknowledge paternity. Or if he doesn't deny he's the father, he may think providing some money will take care of things.

Alexis called the birthfather about her pregnancy. He moved from not believing her to telling her he was sorry and would do anything. Then he called again and said his mother wanted to adopt the baby. Alexis said that wouldn't happen, and from then on he refused to cooperate. Because he would sign no papers, his rights were terminated.

Lisette had broken up with Tom, the birthfather, when she realized she was pregnant. In fact, he was dating a close friend of hers. When he learned about the pregnancy, he offered to provide some money, but said he wanted nothing else to do with the situation. His father was well known in his town and Tom didn't want his parents ever to find out.

Lisette sent him the adoption papers to sign, but he didn't respond. Finally he had to be served the papers, and his parents found out about it. He did sign.

Kernisha felt her baby's father was the loser:

> *The father signed the papers but didn't get involved at all. He wasn't there when Scotty was born. Later he asked me if he could have a picture of his son. I gave it to him because I know he missed out on something wonderful. He has a picture, but no memories of Scotty.*

Reasons for Non-Involvement

One reason a lot of birthfathers don't get involved in adoption planning, according to Sarah Jensen, director, Adoption Center of San Diego, is their feeling of shame at being unable to parent responsibly at this time. "They think people are saying, 'What kind of man are you?'

"I had one recently who said he was too ashamed to meet the adoptive couple. 'How can a man not take care of his own kid?' he asked. I have had other fathers weep because they know adoption is the right thing for their child, but they feel so powerless. I think birthmothers need to try to understand how the men in their lives are feeling. It's hard for both of them," Jensen concluded.

Sometimes a birthfather is against an adoption plan because he truly wants to parent his child. Other birthfathers may not be interested in active parenting. Instead, he may expect either the birthmother or his own mother to do the parenting.

In either case, a good counselor could help him consider his child's needs as well as his own.

Birthfathers Have Rights

What rights should fathers have in adoption planning? What rights *do* fathers have?

Married couples, of course, normally share parental rights. If a married woman wishes to release her baby for adoption, her husband must also sign the legal relinquishment—even if he is not the child's father.

Years ago, an unmarried father's permission was not required if the mother made an adoption plan. Only the mother's signature was needed. Today, however, the father's signature, if he can be found, is almost always required before the adoption can be finalized.

If you are considering an adoption plan, and you aren't with your baby's father, it is extremely important that you know the law in your state or province regarding the father's signature in an adoption. Courts and agencies in most states insist that both parents must consent to the release of their child.

If the father can't be found, agencies usually try to locate him. If they can't find him, the court is petitioned to remove the rights of the absent or unknown father. After a certain period of time, the child can then be released for adoption.

Sometimes a birthmother doesn't want her baby's father even to know she's pregnant. Or she may feel he'd be opposed to the adoption plan. She doesn't want him notified. However, a birthfather may be as concerned about his baby's life as is the birthmother. Shutting the father out of the adoption planning can backfire.

If you're in this situation, you need to know the father's legal rights. You don't want the adoption stopped at some later time because he comes back to demand his rights as the child's other parent. You don't want your child's life disrupted after s/he is living with the adoptive family.

If you don't want to talk with him, perhaps you can help your adoption counselor make an appointment with him. When he realizes the ultimate goal of an adoption plan is to provide a good life for his child, and that he may be part of that planning, he may decide to cooperate fully by signing the relinquishment papers.

If Father Doesn't Sign

Cassandra understands the seriousness of a high-risk placement. Dennis' family was against adoption, but Dennis showed little interest in Cassandra's pregnancy after she refused to have an abortion. He talked to the adoption counselor a few times, and went with Cassandra once to meet the adoptive couple she had selected. Cassandra continues the story:

We met with Margaret and Lee a second time, and he told them he wanted them to raise our baby.

He also talked about how hard this was for him because he was losing his older brothers' respect because each of them had a couple of kids. He wasn't sure he could go through with it.

Dennis said he would sign on his own before the baby was born. He went to the lawyer's office, but he freaked out and he didn't sign.

When Louie was born, Margaret and Lee came to the hospital and saw him right away. Dennis showed up that night during visiting hours, and his mother came over the next day.

Margaret and Lee came back and held Louie for awhile. That was Saturday, and they took him home when I was discharged later that day.

Monday night the adoption counselor called Dennis, and he said, "I've changed my mind. I'm not going to sign."

So they called Margaret and Lee, and they brought Louie back that night. We called our pastor and borrowed a crib. We didn't have anything, no diapers, no clothes, nothing for a baby because we didn't think we'd need it.

I was shocked, like this isn't happening, but I had to deal with it. Margaret and Lee had bought Louie a bunch of clothes. He had already worn some of them, and they gave those to me. We've seen them several times, and they got another baby several months later. I'm happy for them.

We had to get a bunch of stuff. We had to find a babysitter who could start as soon as school started a week after I got home from the hospital.

Dennis was very confused and mostly went with what his mom wanted him to do.

If you're a teenager, it's the rest of your life planned out for you if you have a baby. I have to get a job. I went to visit the college, and a lot of the fuss was on life in the dorm. I'm not going to be able to live in the dorm.

Adoption is a good thing, and it makes a lot of sense right now. Margaret and Lee were going to let me see Louie twice a year plus I'd get letters, and it wasn't like he would go away forever.

Taking care of him is a huge huge responsibility. I look at my friends, and I can't be with them any more.

Looking back, Cassandra discussed some of the issues:

I went to some birthmother support meetings while I was pregnant but I really didn't involve Dennis because they didn't have anything for birthfathers. If they had worked directly with him . . . or if the lawyer hadn't been out of town when Louie was born . . .

Dennis isn't showing any interest in caring for Louie. His mom might, but I don't want that.

Both Birthparents Need to Be Involved

Releasing your baby for adoption will be hard. If you decide adoption is the best plan for you and the baby, you want the process to go smoothly for you and your partner, for your baby, and for the adoptive parents.

The father who does not make a decision creates a difficult situation for the mother—and the baby and potential adoptive parents.

If you have decided on or are thinking about releasing your baby for adoption, check the law in your state or province. If you are married, of course both you and your husband must sign the papers. A number of married couples voluntarily release children for adoption each year, according to adoption statistics. If you are single, carefully check with an adoption agency on the laws concerning fathers' rights in your area. It is important to you—and to your baby—that the adoption occur as smoothly as possible.

It is *extremely* important that *all* legal aspects are handled properly. Also important are the birthfather's needs along with the birthmother's. He may want to be involved equally in the planning for his baby's future. While he doesn't have the physical bond of pregnancy, he may form a strong emotional bond with his child.

If your relationship with the birthfather is over, you still need to try to work with him throughout the adoption planning and placement. Getting him involved in planning a placement ceremony for the time you give your baby to the adoptive parents might help him feel included. This is a hard time for him, too.

Making an adoption plan is difficult, whether you are the birthmother or the birthfather. Whichever you are, do all you can to get the help you and your partner will need to make the best possible plan for your baby, and then to handle the loss of your child to the adoptive family.

It won't be easy for either of you.

CHAPTER **5**

Considering Your Extended Family

It's hard for my family, especially my mom. My mom was my best friend through all of this.

Before I decided to place her for adoption, we had a lot of talks about what having a new grandchild would be like. She was starting to get excited. I was the first daughter to get pregnant, so she was excited for me.

I didn't realize my mom was letting go of a grandchild and my sister was letting go of a niece. When they said good-bye in the hospital it was hard for me to watch them. I wanted my mom and dad there to hold the baby. It was a tear-jerking moment because they were saying good-bye to their grandchild.

My mom was with me when I met the parents, and she wrote a letter to them. I know she has a lot of love for the baby and for that family.

Pati

*My father was very negative toward adoption. He felt
he would be losing a grandchild and he didn't want to
be involved. He wasn't even going to come to the hospital after the birth. I called him and asked him to please
come see the baby.*

*My mother was supportive, but she was also very
ashamed. I think she felt she had failed, that somehow it
was her fault. She wanted the whole thing to be a secret.
None of my family knew, not even my grandparents, until
Jenae's birth.*

*We did tell Grandma and Grandpa at that point. I
hated the fact that we didn't talk to them earlier because
they were close to Kathleen, and I think would have
been a great source of support. But my mom wanted to
sweep it all under the carpet.*

Nick

Adoption Affects Extended Family

Adoption *begins* with birthmothers and birthfathers. It can
lead to the formation of wonderful adoptive families with
continuing ties to the birthparents. Often an adoption plan,
however, affects not only the birthparents, but also their
extended families.

If the birthparent has other children, placing their sibling
with another family can be traumatic for those children. If this
is your situation, being open and honest with the child(ren)
you are parenting is always best. As a starter, you and your
child(ren) can work together to build a relationship with the
family you select.

Julie's daughter was two and her son was eight when she
became pregnant. She was no longer with the father, and she
decided it would be best for herself, her baby, and the two
children she already had if she made an adoption plan. She
talked with a counselor, went over a number of resumes, and
chose Carole and Bob. She reported:

Two weeks after I met Carole and Bob, I took Allan and Karina over for a picnic with them. Carole spent a lot of time with us before I delivered. After the baby was born, the kids and I met with them to sign papers. We've spent time together every month or two ever since.

Karina was too young to understand what was going on, but I explained to Allan that this wasn't very different from his father's other son who never lived with us. I also found several picture books about being adopted, and I read those to the kids.

I really don't think it was a problem for the kids, nor for me either. We had already developed such a good relationship with Carole and Bob, and I was comfortable with it. I think that helped the kids.

Children's reactions depend greatly on their parents' attitudes. Because Julie was positive about her baby's placement with Carole and Bob, her two other children were able to accept the fact that their little brother has another family.

Dealing with Grandparents' Views

In nearly every state, the grandparents of the baby have no legal rights in adoption. Only the birthparents must sign relinquishment papers. Families, however, can make it extremely difficult for a birthparent to go against their wishes in either adoption planning or parenting.

Sometimes the parents feel strongly that their daughter (or son) is not ready to parent. They may feel they, as grandparents, would have to take most of the parenting responsibilities for this child. For good reasons, they may insist that an adoption plan be carried out.

However, if the birthparent feels the adoption plan was made without consideration for her feelings, she is likely to have an especially tough time dealing with the placement. Her grief is likely to be even more intense if she feels the adoption was forced on her. Statistically, she is more likely to be pregnant again within a year or two than she would be if she had placed her child for adoption because *she* considered adoption the wisest choice.

It's a hard question. If you really will not be able to take full responsibility for your child and you are opposed to an adoption plan, there may appear to be no acceptable solution. You know that neither adoption nor parenting would be easy for you and your child's other parent.

Your best bet under these circumstances is to learn all you can about parenting *and* about adoption. Look beyond the wonders of a tiny baby to parenting a toddler, a preschooler, even a teenager. Figure out the degree of help you would have to have. How much are your parents or other family members willing to supply?

While she was pregnant, Katelynn didn't feel her parents were as supportive as she'd have liked. She commented:

> *I stayed in college the year I was pregnant, but I went home for the summer. I think it was hard for my parents to deal with because they worried about what people would think. They didn't like people making gossipy comments behind my back.*
>
> *They let me know from the beginning that they would support me emotionally, but I couldn't expect financial support. That bothered me at the time, but now I realize I should never have expected them to parent my child. That was my responsibility.*

You may decide that, within your reality at this time, parenting would not be the best plan, given your family's lack of support. Or you may be able to figure out a realistic plan for working out the many details of parenting without depending on your parents or anyone else for support.

Taylor was president of her class and very involved in sports and band when she realized she was pregnant. She understood the impact her pregnancy had on her family:

*My family was well-known in town, and it was tough
telling them. I disappointed my parents a great deal, but
the first thing they said was, "We're here for you. We'll
support you in whatever you decide to do."*

*They had a hard time, especially during the first half
of my pregnancy. They didn't want to be seen with me.*

*I visited with three different counselors, working on
decision-making. I know it was hard for my family to
keep their mouths shut and let me make the decision.*

*When I was about eight months pregnant, we had a
family meeting — which I think is a good plan for other
families, too. They all took turns talking about how they
felt about my pregnancy, and talking about my options. I
think I had gotten pretty self-absorbed and wasn't
thinking about their feelings. This meeting helped me
realize how this was affecting them.*

Grandparents Grieve Loss of Grandchild

If you are planning an adoption, your parents may go along
with your decision throughout pregnancy. If they don't talk
about it, you—and they—may assume it won't be a problem
for them. When you deliver, however, they may find the
adoption placement far more difficult for them than they had
anticipated. When you see your child, the impact this wonderful grandchild has on them may be overwhelming.

*The adoption was very hard on my parents and my
grandma. I'm the only child, and this was their first
grandchild—and my grandma's first great-grandchild. I
think the whole house went through a post-partum
depression after the baby was gone.*

*I talk to my mom about it a lot. They really had a
hard time, but they love Tony and Darlene. That helps.*

Kernisha

Maggie appreciated her mother's support of her adoption
plan. She didn't realize until after delivery how difficult it was

for her mom to deal with the coming loss of her grandchild:

> *My mom and I dealt with it by joking. She was 42,*
> *and I would say, "Right, mom, you're going to be a*
> *grandma. You realize how old that makes you?"*
>
> *She would say, "I refuse to be a grandma. You can't*
> *call me that."*
>
> *Strangely enough, we never really talked about how*
> *she was feeling through all this. I guess I never thought*
> *about it.*
>
> *Then the night Jessica was born, my mom and a*
> *friend went to the store to buy me ice cream. My friend*
> *said my mom walked up to the checker and said, "Guess*
> *what? I'm a grandma!" That meant a lot to me.*

Sometimes at this point parents who firmly supported an adoption plan say, "You can keep him. We will help you. We can do it together."

You would be wise to consider this possibility *before* you deliver. The hours after childbirth are a very emotional time. This is *not* the time to make life-changing decisions.

The best approach is to encourage your parents to get counseling during your pregnancy. Perhaps you can help them understand that this baby is their grandchild. While it's your decision whether to place for adoption or parent yourself, they may need help in accepting your decision. They, too, will grieve the loss of your child.

They, too, however, want their grandchild to have the best possible life. Is there a grandparent support group they could attend? Talking with even one other birthgrandparent might help them sort out their feelings on this issue. Perhaps your parents say they will support you in whatever decision you make. That's good, but at the same time, they need to face their own feelings.

Sometimes it's a sibling of the birthparent who is most hurt by the pregnancy and the loss of the baby:

*I think my brother was the most heartbroken. He was
11, and he really didn't understand what was going on.
He saw my daughter, but he was afraid to ask me anything about it for fear he would say the wrong thing.
He's 21 now, and we talk about it a lot. He kept it inside
for a long time, and that made it harder for him.*

Tatum

Support Group for Birthgrandparents

Wendy Heiser, Bethany Christian Services, Seattle, Washington, realizes the struggle grandparents may have during
adoption planning and after placement.

"Some birthmoms bring their parents in for visits and we
sit and talk," she said. "Sometimes I refer them to a
birthgrandparent support group because I know it's healthy
for them to talk about this grandchild. They have a lot of
disappointment in their own child for letting this happen, and
for losing their grandchild.

"Sometimes it's hard for the birthmom to deal with it if her
parents are struggling with her decision. Parents are supposed
to be strong for the birthmother," she concluded.

*A week or two after Jessica's birth, my mom said,
"I'm sorry if you felt I wasn't there for you. I just felt I
didn't want to get attached. I thought if I didn't think
about it or talk about it, I wouldn't get attached." But
the second Jessica was born, she couldn't help herself.*

*I think it's been hitting her the past couple of years.
She's getting to the place where she wants to have
grandchildren.*

*I still keep in touch with the birthfather's parents,
Jessica's birthgrandparents. They were very close and
wanted to be a part of her life. I make copies of the
pictures and letters for them.*

*He got married last year and has a child now. Per-
haps that's why he's finally starting to ask his mom*

about Jessica. She told me she showed him her pictures
just the other day.

Maggie

Some Families Won't Talk About Adoption

Some parents will not talk about the adoption because of
their continuing feelings about their daughter's pregnancy.
Yvette placed her baby four years ago. She can talk about her
child to her mother, but not to her father:

My mom brings it up, and I know I can go to her and
talk about it. I don't mention it to my father because he
doesn't say much about it. I was his baby, and I changed
my whole life. That almost destroyed him at the time.
He's okay, but I don't think he likes to talk about it.

My brother has a little girl about Rosie's age. He
married her mother, and he thinks I did the right thing.
He tells me, "It's hard with both parents trying to work
and give her everything she needs. It takes a lot of time
and money. You did the right thing, thinking about your
child and yourself."

In some families, the unwillingness to talk about the
adoption stems from total opposition to the fact of
placement:

My family wanted no contact with me. We didn't talk
until a year after I placed my baby, and I'm still the only
person that talks about the adoption. If I bring it up,
everybody gets real quiet. Nobody acknowledges that
she exists although I have pictures of her on my
refrigerator.

My grandmother didn't like the idea at all. She
figured if she could do it, I could. But I knew I wasn't
ready to parent. I wanted my child to have a stable
family.

Jazmin

Your pregnancy may be a hard reality for your family to face. Perhaps if they don't think about the baby as their grandchild, they won't hurt so much. Chances are great, however, that the hurt will come, perhaps right after your baby is born, or maybe it will be months or even years down the road. Getting involved in counseling and/or a support group could help.

A book your parents might find helpful is *Parents, Pregnant Teens and the Adoption Option: Help for Families* (1989: Morning Glory Press). It includes many suggestions from birthgrandparents on dealing first with a daughter's untimely pregnancy, and second, with the loss of a grandchild through adoption.

If you are young and dependent on your family, it's probably even more important that you look at both your parenting and your adoption options. If you decide to go against your family's preference, you will need to be extra firm in your decision.

Your pregnancy has changed your life. Those changes will have a big impact on your family, too. If you can continue to communicate with each other, care about each other, and love each other, you will have a better chance of making the best possible decision for your baby and for you.

CHAPTER **6**

Counseling —
Why? When? How?

I hadn't thought adoption would be such an emotional experience. I didn't think I could make it through, but I did. I'm still healing, but I'm doing well.

I needed the agency. They worked with me and wanted me to express my feelings. I lived at the home and they brought in children who had been adopted. We would talk with them.

My mom told me a year ago that I'm the most unselfish person in the world. "You gave up something that meant so much to you," she said. She was right.

Yvette

Counseling made me think about issues, like what I was going to do after she was born. Even more effective was talking with someone who had been in my situation.

Katelynn

Adoption Agency Can Help

Many young women and couples unintentionally pregnant
talk to adoption agency counselors simply because they want
to talk to someone. They may not plan to place their babies
for adoption, but they know a counselor can help them sort
out their feelings and concerns.

If you're worried about an unplanned pregnancy, or you
aren't quite sure of your decision regarding your child's
future, you can talk things over with a trained counselor. Look
in the yellow pages of your telephone book under "Adoption."
You'll probably find one or more listings if you live in an
urban area. You can also contact your state or local child
welfare agency for information.

You don't need to accept the services of the first agency or
adoption center you contact. In fact, you're probably better off
researching several. Jazmin called an agency in her home
town, but soon realized this was not the place for her:

> They really grilled me, and I was upset. I had heard
> good things about them, but one of the first things they
> asked was what race my baby was. When I said he
> would be mixed, they said they didn't have a place for
> him, that they only place white children. I almost
> decided not to call anyone else.
>
> But I called an agency in another city. When I told
> them my baby is mixed with black and I'm Puerto Rican,
> they said, "No problem. We place a lot of babies of
> mixed race."
>
> I said, "Is that for real? I don't want my baby running
> from foster home to foster home," and they assured me
> there were homes waiting.

Adoption Is Traumatic

Adoption is a traumatic event for birthparents *and* adoptive
parents. Each parent faces loss.

The birthparents lose their baby. In the old days of

confidential adoption, this was sometimes compared to losing a child through death, except there was no grave, no mourning, no funeral, no memorial service.

The adoptive parents must face the loss of their dream of creating a biological family. Adoption is a fine way to build a family, but it is not the same as biological birth. Often, the adoptive parents have endured infertility treatments, perhaps for years, with no success. Finally, when they turn to adoption as a possible way of building their family, they benefit from professional counseling, too.

Going directly to an attorney for adoption help can be risky for the adoptive parents because of the typical lack of counseling. It can be even riskier for the birthparents for the same reason. In addition, the adoptive parents are paying the attorney, making them his primary clients. Might this interfere with his concern for the birthparents?

Some attorneys understand the importance of counseling, especially for birthparents. Deborah Crouse Cobb, Edwardsville, Illinois, is an adoption attorney who firmly believes in counseling. "When I have teenage clients," she said, "I strongly push the counseling because it's too easy for them to be pressured by their mothers or their peers. I can't pressure older women into counseling. When they say adamantly that they don't want it, I can't force them. But I do put it in the record that if she needs counseling later, the adoptive parents will pay for it."

Many of the birthmothers who don't want counseling come back later, often about the time of the baby's first birthday, according to Cobb. They are in denial. They are grieving, and they don't understand it. "Why do I feel this grief and loss?" they ask. "This is what I wanted." Nobody helped them prepare for these emotions, and after awhile they can't live with it.

"I've never had a problem with adoptive parents refusing to pay for the counseling a year later," Cobb stated.

Choosing an Adoption Counselor

Generally, you're more assured of getting professional
counseling when you work with an agency. If the counselor
appears to suggest you should (or should not) place your child
for adoption, look for a different counselor. Counselors are
not supposed to give you answers—that's not their job. They
are supposed to help you sort out your feelings and guide you
toward making the best decisions for you and your baby.

> *The birthparent counselor helped us prepare for*
> *placement. Talking with her really helped me with my*
> *decision. From the first time I walked in and spoke to*
> *Marilyn, there was so much about that agency that made*
> *me feel comfortable with my decision.*
>
> *There was no pressure there. That had been my*
> *biggest fear, that somebody would sit me down and say,*
> *"You should do this." This was not what I wanted.*
>
> *Instead, we talked about my options, what my needs*
> *were, how they could help. Marilyn said they were there*
> *to help me but not to make my decision. You have to*
> *trust your instincts. If you feel threatened, if you feel*
> *they are trying to pressure you, you don't want that.*
>
> *Marilyn talked with Steve and me separately once or*
> *twice, but generally we were there together.*
>
> Sabrina

Whether you work with an agency or not, it's important to
find a counselor trained in adoption counseling. Sonia soon
realized her psychologist wasn't providing the kind of help
she needed:

> *I saw a psychologist before delivery, but he didn't*
> *think I needed counseling. He didn't know anything*
> *about adoption.*
>
> Sonia

Professional counseling is important and can help you deal
with the feelings you'll have if you make an adoption plan.

A good counselor will help you look at your needs and your choices. Then you make the decisions.

The counselor/facilitator you choose is an extremely important part of your adoption planning. You don't want someone who, for a fee, simply "matches" adoptive and birthparents without knowing anything about either party. You don't want someone whose main goal is to place your baby with another family. An important question to ask is "What happens if I decide to parent my child myself?" No facilitator should ever try to talk you into placing your child with another family. This is strictly your decision.

Discussing Options with Counselor

Birthparents can expect an adoption counselor to help them examine their options thoroughly. As discussed before, people considering an adoption plan generally are wise to consider a parenting plan as well. Comparing the plus and minus factors in each, she/they can make a better decision for their child.

If you decide to parent your child, your counselor should help you consider those realities. S/he can probably help you contact community resources you may need in order to develop parenting skills and to plan your life with your baby. If adoption is your choice, your counselor will probably ask if you are ready to let go of your parenting relationship with your child. Are you choosing adoption because it's the right decision *for you,* or simply because you think it's what you ought to do?

Your counselor can also help you with your plans for after the placement of your child. You'll need to have supportive and caring people there for you, and you need to have plans for your own life.

> *The counseling at my agency was great. We did a lot of in-depth counseling. I had been abused as a child, mentally and physically, and Carolyn helped me deal with those issues. We also had group therapy.*

It was nice to have counseling after I placed. Any time I want to go there and talk, she puts aside a few minutes and we can talk about anything.

I've had friends go through different agencies who placed, and didn't get the counseling they needed. It makes a big difference in how you handle the pain.

Jazmin

Talking with Other Birthparents

For many people, talking with family members or friends is a valuable part of decision-making. If those family members and those friends have never placed a child for adoption, however, they probably cannot truly empathize with your situation. Sometimes it's more help to talk to someone who has been there.

Talking with someone who had been through an adoption helped me the most. I felt like if I parted from my baby I would never have a normal life again. It was the hardest decision I ever made, of course, but through talking with another birthmother, I knew I wouldn't be insane the rest of my life.

This woman has two children, is married, and is happy. We talked the whole time I was pregnant. She was my support system because she had been in my shoes.

Katelynn

Footprints Program Offers Mentors

Carole Adlard, Adoption Option Inc., Cincinnati, Ohio, developed the Footprints Program to meet this need to talk to other birthparents. About 50 individuals have volunteered as mentors.

When someone calls Adoption Option concerning pregnancy decision-making, that person is given a packet of information about adoption. In addition, the individual or couple is offered a mentor, someone to talk with, a friend who will understand her feelings because the mentor has already dealt with similar feelings.

"We prefer to work with birthcouples when possible," Adlard explained. "Each receives a mentor, and we try to match each person up with someone who has had similar experiences—a woman with a bi-racial pregnancy with someone else in that situation; someone who has been raped with someone else who has experienced this trauma. Some end up being good friends. It depends on what each wants.

"For one person, it may be a need simply for someone to talk with, but not go out together. Someone else may prefer a mentor who will go shopping and to the movies with her. The key element here is respect. The purpose is to meet the needs of the birthparents. Footprints is for those who want to learn about adoption first-hand."

> *I think a support group is important. I'm glad my friends and family were there, but they couldn't really understand.*
>
> *Now I'm a volunteer with Footprints. I talked with Kernisha before and after she placed, and I think that helped her. I wish I had had something like Footprints.*
>
> *I'm an advocate of counseling, but it's not going to help someone who's not ready for it. I didn't really think about it before I placed. Even afterward I didn't talk to other birthmothers about it. I wish I had.*
>
> Maggie

Pre-Placement Grieving Helps

Sometimes birthparents don't think they really need counseling—until later:

> *Actually I felt the counseling sessions were a waste of time when I was there. I thought to myself, why are we talking about this? I didn't want to talk about it. I think now that I wasn't ready to face it.*

Afterward I was glad we had talked about the sadness I'd be feeling. Immediately after placing I was so glad to have someone there I could talk to weekly. I was real grateful for that.

That first year is a doozie, and unless you have something or someone else that can totally consume your attention, it's got to be one of the hardest years you can possibly imagine. I saw the counselor for nearly a year after placement. I discovered I needed her.

Tatum

Janet Fish, Marywood Children and Family Services, Austin, Texas, talked about their counseling process. "We encourage our clients to see us at least two months before delivery, preferably sooner," she said. "We want to help them work through the grief process so they don't have to deal so much with that when they face the trauma of the birth. We help them understand the feelings they will have, and most of them start that process before delivery.

"Of course we see them after delivery and after placement. We have monthly birthparent support groups, and they come as long as they wish. We don't see much mind-changing after delivery, and I think that's partly because of this preparation," she said.

Lisette lived at Marywood during part of her pregnancy:

Marywood is big on going through a grieving process while you're pregnant. But I didn't want to do much grieving because I didn't want my child to feel I was unhappy because then he would be unhappy. I had this white teddy bear, and it fit right over my belly. I got the baby one just like it, and his parents said he would sleep with his head on it.

During those three months I really thought my decision through. Keeping the baby crossed my mind a few times, but I'm pretty stubborn and I didn't change my mind.

In open adoption, it may be even more important for birthparents and adoptive parents to be able to go back to the adoption facilitator for counseling. Either the birth or the adoptive parents (or both) may decide changes are needed in the initial contact agreement. Sometimes it helps to have an uninvolved person helping with the negotiations for such a change. Open adoption is a life-long process, and feelings about this process may change over time.

As before, the counselor's role is not to set new rules of contact. If the old ones appear to need changing, her role is to help the adoptive parents and the birthparents work together on the development of new guidelines to meet *their* needs.

If Your Peers Are Opposed to Adoption

Making an adoption plan may be especially hard if you are with other pregnant women every day, women who are planning to parent their children. This often happens when a teenager enrolls in a special school program for pregnant students.

Many of the young women in the class may be planning to rear their children themselves. In fact, they may be quite opposed to the idea of adoption. They may make comments such as "How can you give your baby away?" or "Don't you love your baby?"

If you're in this kind of group, realize first that many of your peers don't feel they have the choice to place their child for adoption. Their parents or their boyfriend may be completely opposed to adoption. Or they may simply be uninformed about the whole process. In any case, their thoughtless comments are likely to mask their feelings of insecurity about their approaching parenting responsibilities. Sonia was in this situation:

I was attending a teen parent school program, and half the girls thought I was making a mistake. Going there made me want to give him up even more. I saw

them with their children, and what parenting at that
point was doing to their lives.

I decided on adoption one day when I took a walk in
the park. I was holding my stomach and feeling the baby
move inside me. I was thinking about my life and what I
could give him. I knew I didn't want my parents to raise
him, and I thought, "I have to think of you first. I have to
give you up because that will be better for you, and it
will be better for me, too."

I knew at that point that baby wasn't mine. I loved
him so much—I had to do that for him. I didn't know
much about adoption, but I knew what I wanted to do.

A lot of people tried to talk me out of it. At first my
parents didn't like the idea. They said they would help
me raise him, but then they realized it was my decision.

I knew I wasn't ready to be a mother, a good mother.

Discussing Adoption with Pregnant Teens

If you're in a pregnant teen class, ask your teacher if there
will be any discussion of adoption. Your classmates need
information about adoption for several reasons. Some may be
adoptees themselves, and they need to understand the tremen-
dous love that goes into an adoption decision. Others might
consider an adoption plan for their babies if they become
informed about today's adoption practices. And, of course,
with a little information about adoption, they might be more
supportive of your decision to consider an adoption plan.

Sonia discussed this issue:

There was no class session on adoption. I think it
would have been better for the girls to be prepared
that I was coming. Adoption should be discussed
because a lot of them never even thought about it. It
would also help them respect a birthmother's decision.

Don't let anybody tell you what to do. If you have just
one person who supports you, lean on that person. I was

*lucky because I had a lot of support. You have to do
what you believe is right. Don't let somebody else tell
you what to do. They aren't you.*

TARGET Helps Teens Consider Options

Marywood, Austin, Texas, is a maternity home with a dual
purpose. For many years they specialized in adoption, and if a
couple came to Marywood, they were thinking adoption.

"Now we have another program, a 30-day intense therapeu-
tic program," Janet Fish explained. "It's for young women
either planning on parenting or who want to explore options,
or are perhaps quite confused. We help them refocus their
goals and take a long hard look at their future and their baby's
future. We help them think about how to meet those goals,
whether or not they choose adoption."

TARGET (Teens at Risk Getting Essentials Together) is a
residential program designed for young women in their
second trimester of pregnancy. TARGET clients stay thirty
days, and during that time they research their options thoroughly. There is no pressure to choose the adoption option,
only to plan carefully for their child's future, whether they
eventually release for adoption or parent themselves. Last
year one in four TARGET clients came back for the adoption
placement program.

If she is planning to parent, she goes home for the last
trimester armed with skills to look at the realities of her
environment and make realistic plans for herself and her baby.

"We only accept TARGET clients who want to be there.
It's been a great program with absolutely no pressure to
place," Fish said. Family counseling is an important part of
the program.

Loryna, 16, attended the TARGET program at Marywood:

*After I got out of the TARGET program, I had pretty
much decided on adoption. My parents wouldn't talk
about it, but I moved in with my grandparents and they*

were totally supportive.

*Before I picked out the parents, the counselor made
me write a baby letter, a letter the adoptive parents will
give to my baby when she's old enough to understand
why I placed her for adoption. That letter was real hard
to write because I hadn't separated from my child yet. I
told my counselor she must be crazy—I couldn't write a
letter to my baby when she wasn't even gone yet. But I
did, and it was pretty good.*

Adoptive Parents Pay Counseling Fees

Adoptive parents pay fees covering a portion of the cost of
counseling services to them and to the birthparent(s) both
before and after adoption. Fees are usually on a sliding scale
based on the adoptive couple's income. The fee includes cost
of services to the family and the child after placement.

In some states an agency cannot provide financial assistance to the birthmother, but the social worker should be able
to refer you to others who will give you the help you need.

If you do decide on adoption, the agency will take care of
all the legal aspects. They stay informed on new legislation
and are very aware of your needs. They want whatever is best
for you.

Nick and Kathleen started seeing a counselor about four
months into the pregnancy. The counseling, which Kathleen's
parents pushed, dealt more with their relationship than with
adoption planning.

Kathleen's grandmother offered them books and a video on
adoption. As they learned about adoption, they decided they
wanted to investigate further. They started meeting with a
social worker from the Children's Home in their city. They
went to support group meetings, too. Nick explained:

*That's how Kathleen's mother believed in dealing
with problems. You educate yourself, speak with people,
read books. We were influenced by her family a great*

*deal. As a boyfriend with a child on the way, I felt my
role was to be supportive and to be involved in whatever
process she wanted to go through.*

*I think it was very beneficial to have an outsider's
viewpoint. Family members are likely to have opinions
and to tell you what you ought to do. These people were
there to give us helpful suggestions and, most important,
listen. That helped us deal with the pregnancy. I suggest
that anyone going through this process talk to people.*

Counseling Issues Explored

Nancy Johnson, Spokane Consultants in Family Living,
Spokane, Washington, prefers to see birthmothers at least ten
times before the baby is born. "We talk about her stresses, her
issues, her relationship with her mom," she said. "We talk
about her decision-making style. I ask, 'Do you talk it over
with other people? Do you go over it yourself? How do you
make choices?'"

People who have already experienced great hurt, according
to Johnson, "don't back away from this stuff. Those who
haven't already experienced hurt have a harder time with it.
We talk about how she grieves, how she wants to grieve.

"Part of being okay is acting okay," Johnson added. "I tell
them life is about making decisions and then deciding how we
will live with that decision. I think a lot of this is how we deal
with any of the hits in life. We turn left and we turn right, and
a lot of it is what we make of those choices.

"I like to use this relinquishment work as part of living. It's
not a carved-out niche that once you do it, you're damaged for
life," she concluded.

Talking with a good counselor can help you formulate a
plan for your child. Whether you're making an adoption plan
or a parenting plan, counseling can help you develop the best
plan for you and for your child.

Developing an Adoption Plan

I talked with several counselors. I read a lot of books and magazine articles. I talked with other people, both those who were parenting and some who placed for adoption. I also went down to Social Services. They were quite rude to me, but I needed to find out what kind of social assistance would be available to me.

I also made a parenting plan. I was always thinking about both parenting and adoption. I made lists of what I'd need, what kind of mother I'd be, the life I wanted my child to have. I did a lot of journaling as well. I struggled all the way up to the time Crissy was born.

The day she was born was the most wonderful day of my life—and one of the most frightening because I had not made a decision yet. Sometimes I wished I could be pregnant forever so Crissy could stay with me.

Taylor

Planning for Your Child

If you, whether you're with your partner or not, intend to parent your child, you are probably doing a great deal of planning. Where will you live? Will you have help in caring for your baby? Do you have enough money for food, clothes, toys, all the expenses involved in parenting? You need to be sure you have insurance to cover your child's health needs. If you're in school or working, who will care for your child when you aren't home?

Many parents have a wonderful time planning for the coming baby. For some, this is an especially happy time.

For others, the timing is off. This is *not* a good time in their lives to be parenting. If this is true for you, you probably *want* to parent your child. You would love to do all that other planning so necessary for parents-to-be.

If you're thinking of releasing your child to another family to rear, does this mean you don't have to plan? That you can simply coast along, get through pregnancy, and know that your baby will go to a wonderful family without any effort on your part? *Of course not.*

Adoption requires a plan just as parenting requires a plan. In fact, even if you think you've made a rather firm decision already, you'd be wise to consider both plans.

> *I went back and forth during my entire pregnancy. I lived in a small home for pregnant women. It was really hard because people would say, "Well, have you made your decision? Are you sure you're going to keep?"*
>
> *"Well . . ." It was real complicated. A 12-year-old was living there when I was, and her parents were forcing her to place. She was pregnant again about a year after she placed.*
>
> *Another lady was in her late 40s. She already had three kids and she couldn't afford another child. She told me about the struggles she was going through, and the things I needed to be prepared to face. The more I*

*learned about the pregnancy, adoption plans, what
happens afterward, speaking to people who placed, who
had adopted children . . . the more information I got, the
better I felt.*

*I was real afraid those first few months because I
didn't know anything. I was under the impression that
they immediately take your baby, and you don't even
know if it's a boy or a girl. The more I learned that that
was not going to happen, the more I was able to concen-
trate on having a healthy pregnancy. That helped a lot.*

*But the most help came from talking to children who
were adopted. Who better to tell you about adoption
than a child who has been adopted? Talking to those
kids helped me make the right decision.*

*You need to get as much information as you possibly
can about every aspect of all the options, because each
case is different. The more accurate information you can
get, the less afraid you'll be. I was grateful that my
mother gave me complete control over my decision.*

*That last day I called my mother and literally begged
her to make the decision for me. She told me she could
not do it. Parents need to tell the teen, "You really need
to make this decision. Whatever it is, I'll stand by you."*

Tatum

Independent or Agency Adoption

Two kinds of adoption services are available—agency and
independent. In agency adoption, birthparents relinquish
(surrender, release) their child to the adoption agency. The
agency then places the child with a carefully selected family,
a family already approved for placement of a child by
the agency.

Agencies, which may be public or private, sectarian
(church-related) or non-sectarian, usually select their adoptive
families carefully. Families who apply for a healthy baby
through an agency often must wait several years for a baby.

Independent adoption means, by definition, an adoption in which the birthparents select the adoptive family. They place their child directly with that family. A few states do not allow independent placement of children, but most do.

To make the independent placement legal, the birthparents sign a "consent to adoption." This names the specific couple with whom their child is placed. In nearly every state this consent must be signed in the presence of a representative of the State Department of Social Services or its local designee.

If birthparents decide to "go independent," it is important that they consult a reputable lawyer. When birthparents relinquish to an agency, the agency takes care of all the legal matters for them. In an independent adoption, birthparents are *on their own*—unless they choose to work with an independent adoption service. Legal help is essential whether the baby goes to relatives or to strangers.

In some states, the adoptive family is not studied to determine its fitness to adopt the child until *after* the baby is already in their home. At that time, after they already have the child, the couple files an adoption petition in court. The state agency must study them to decide if they are fit to have this baby. Will they love him and provide a good family life for him? Is the child suitable for this particular family?

The state agency also interviews the birthparents to learn about family background, medical history, etc. This information is given to the adoptive family to share with the child.

Choosing Someone to Work with You

Whether you choose an agency or independent adoption plan, working with a good counselor/facilitator is important to you—and, therefore, to your child.

An adoption facilitator is sometimes called an *intermediary* because his/her role, in addition to helping you make a good decision for yourself and your child, is to act as a go-between for you and the adoptive parents. Your facilitator should

provide you with a group of descriptions of possible adoptive
parents, and will encourage you to make a choice based on
your needs. If you are told you shouldn't know the full name
and address of the parents you select, and/or future communication must go through the facilitator, what are they hiding? If
you don't like secrets, be up-front about your wishes.

In fact, it is wise to exchange Social Security numbers.
Then, if you or the adoptive parents should move, you won't
lose track of each other.

It's important you find a facilitator you trust, someone with
whom you can be comfortable as you explore various possi-
bilities. Interview counselors at several agencies and adoption
services.

Ask them what they do. Do they simply hand you a bunch
of paperwork? Or do they look at your needs first? Sometimes
it may feel as though they are interested only in your child.
Your child is important, but so are you. Birthparent counselors
need to be birthparent focused.

*The first place I visited seemed to focus on the
adoptive parents first, and then on me. What I heard
there was the opposite of what I thought open adoption
was. She told me they screen all their clients. I asked,
"Is it possible for me to look at their home studies and
see them before and after they have the baby?"*

She said, "Oh no, I don't think we want to do that."

*I asked her what would happen if the birthmother
changed her mind at the last minute just before the
papers were signed. I got the idea she would see that as
a failure, rather than a choice a birthparent has every
right to make, to parent her child.*

*They were calling it an open adoption because I
could get letters and pictures, but all this had to go
through the agency. I went away from that meeting
terrified that that was the only option out there.*

> *Then I went to see Nancy, and she was totally differ-*
> *ent. She has always said, "If you decide to parent, we're*
> *100 percent behind you. This happens, and the adoptive*
> *parents will get over it."*
>
> Danielle

Both the birthparents and the adoptive parents are likely to appreciate follow-up counseling. You want someone who will be there for you after the adoption is finalized.

You may also want someone there to help you work out any future changes in the contact agreement you and the adoptive parents develop.

Lois Ruskie Melina and Sharon Kaplan Roszia, authors of *The Open Adoption Experience* (1993: Harper Perennial), stress the importance of having plenty of time to make your adoption plan. You and the adoptive parents need time to prepare for the transfer of parental roles. You need to understand each other's concerns and respect each other's boundaries.

Developing a Designer Adoption

If you're considering an adoption plan, one of the most important things is that you feel you're in control, according to Wendy Heiser, Bethany Christian Services, Seattle, Washington. Because of the openness now typical of adoption plans, birthparents can have much more flexibility.

> *Once Nick and I made the decision, it was like I went*
> *into the "Go" mode—we're going to do this. I read all*
> *the books I could find on adoption. The counselor and I*
> *talked, and Nick and I started reading letters from*
> *couples.*
>
> *The process was definitely painful, but there was*
> *some excitement—looking at the choices in parents,*
> *knowing I had some power.*
>
> Kathleen

Educating people on their choices in adoption is the goal of Adoption Options, Cincinnati, Ohio, according to Carole Adlard, director. "We call them designer adoptions because the birthparents create unique situations," she explained. "When you empower birthparents and adoptive parents, the end product is different in each case. There can be so much flexibility. The adoption plan can reflect their values, whatever would be best for them and for their child," she said.

Danielle agrees with the designer adoption concept:

When you're making an adoption plan, you need first to get in your mind what kind of adoption you might want. I think we're a little more closed than some people would want. We don't want to go over every weekend. If we had wanted that, we could have found it. I think open adoption should be just what you make it, and there should not be limits. Some people aren't comfortable with lots of contact, and others need that.

Once you have an idea of what you want, you find an agency that will work with you. Find out if they have any kind of legal contract on the openness. (Danielle lives in a state which provides legal support for open adoption agreements.) *Then take advantage of every service the agency provides—one-on-one counseling, group counseling, etc.*

Look at every option. For me, it was trying not to get carried away in the romantic view of "Oh, I'm going to have this little baby and it will be perfect." Look at your life, what it is now, and what it would be like if you parent.

We were trying to be adult, and we would have had to go on welfare or take money from our parents if we'd kept our baby. We wanted to be adults before we parented a child.

As you consider an adoption plan, think about the degree of

openness you might want with the adoptive family. If you
want to continue contact after placement, you need to find an
agency or independent adoption center that will help you
work out that kind of plan.

Researching Adoption Plans and Facilitators

Before you decide on an intermediary, whether an agency,
attorney, or independent adoption facilitator, shop around.
Find someone who can meet *your* needs. You need the best
services you can find.

Alexis, 18, started out with the idea of talking with several
people about adoption. She understood that she didn't need to
depend on the first agency or adoption facilitator she met:

> *My mom taught me to shop around, compare prices. I
> did the same thing with adoption. I called several
> places. One agency was real closed and said I couldn't
> visit after my child was placed. The second place wasn't
> much better. I wanted to pick the best parents I could,
> and I wanted to make sure my child was okay, so the
> adoption needed to be open. And I didn't think it was
> right at all that the agency had control. I thought, how
> can you guys put a restraint on my love for my child?*
>
> *The next place I went said they did open adoptions,
> but they wouldn't let me see a lot of files. Then I went to
> see an attorney. He explained things, but I was turned
> off because it wasn't a very loving atmosphere. Doing
> family work in an attorney's office didn't seem right.*
>
> *Next I went to an independent adoption center, and I
> decided they offered what I wanted. I went back, and
> they gave me a whole stack of files.*

Annette made the heart-wrenching decision to place her
four-year-old for adoption only after doing careful research on
her options:

> *I talked with several places. I explained my situation*

and asked, "What kind of care will my child get? Can I help choose the parents? Would I be able to visit him?"

One place said once I placed Isaac I could receive letters but could have no contact with him. I said definitely no. Another place told me I probably would be able to see him once a year, depending on how the adoptive family felt. But I wouldn't get to choose the family because they didn't think it was safe for a mother to see the parents and know where they were.

I wanted to be sure my son didn't end up with a weirdo. I needed to know who these people were. I didn't want someone from out of state even though I realized anyone could move after they adopted him.

Finally I called another agency for more information, and they wanted to help me. I decided this was what I had to do, and Isaac went to the foster family. After he had been there awhile, I asked if they would adopt him, and they said they would. They'd already been thinking about it.

They are bright people, real talkative. When I see them, they hug me and I feel like I'm part of the family. It's a black family, church people, a real decent family.

We had the placement ceremony a couple of months ago. I see Isaac every three months now.

Whether you work with an attorney, an agency, or independent adoption facilitator, find out what happens if you decide to parent. Will the intermediary be there to help you work through that decision? Some agencies and other adoption services are designed to help their clients whether they make an adoption or a parenting plan.

Make sure you have an advocate working for *you.*

It's best to interview several people before you choose someone to work with you. You do have choices. A lot of people are waiting to parent children, and there are also many people wanting to work with pregnant families. Sadly, some of these people "match" birthparents and adoptive parents mainly as a money-making business. You know that choosing another family for your child is not a business decision. It's a decision of the heart and mind.

The people working in adoption need to be paid fairly for their services, but not all of them are concerned with the welfare of the birthfamily. When you're shopping for an adoption intermediary, ask for their credentials. Is this person a licensed therapist, someone who is working with an agency or an attorney? If someone offers to match you with an adoptive couple without knowing anything about you, you should be concerned. They may not know much about the adoptive couple either.

Even if you think you don't want counseling, insist that it be available if you want it later. Also ask about preparation of potential adoptive parents. If you want an open adoption, you need to find parents who understand how and are willing to have this kind of adoption.

If you don't know much about the intermediary you're considering, you can call your state's Social Services Department Adoptions Division. Say, "I'm planning to place my child for adoption, and these are some programs or individuals I might work with. Have there been any lawsuits or complaints? Or have they been under investigation for anything underhanded?" You might get some helpful information.

Preparing Adoptive Parents

In many agencies and independent adoption services, prospective adoptive parents attend one or more group meetings with other would-be parents. At these meetings they learn about the children waiting for adoption. They explore their own reasons for wanting to adopt a child. They also learn more about the process of adoption.

Often, an important part of these group meetings involves adoptive parents meeting, talking with, and hearing the stories

of birthparents. Adoptive parents who don't know any
birthparents may not understand the pain involved in releasing
a child for adoption.

Sometimes adoptive parents fear the unknown birthparents,
thinking they might return for their child. Simply talking with
birthparents helps a would-be adoptive couple develop empa-
thy for their future adopted child's birthparents.

> *A lot of people have all these fears, both birthmothers
> and adoptive parents. People often make decisions
> based on their fears, but when they talk to people, the
> fears tend to go away. It's like prejudice anywhere.*
>
> *At first, open adoption is hard, but in the long run, it's
> easier. We wanted Betsy to have a relationship with her
> birthparent, and that's what Alexis wanted, too. We don't
> necessarily want her in our lives every day, but we
> wanted more than a Christmas card.*
>
> *We know Betsy is ahead knowing her birthmom.*
>
> Cynthia, adoptive mother

In most agencies, after the adoptive couple fills out a
lengthy application form, a social worker meets with the
couple together and separately, and visits them in their home.
Topics discussed usually include the adoptive couple's reasons for wanting to adopt a child, the strength of their marriage, their attitudes toward childrearing, their financial
stability, and their capabilities for parenting a child born to
someone else.

Basically, the agency is looking for the kind of parents you
would like your child to have if you decide you want someone
else to raise him/her. They want couples who have a stable
home life where a child will fit in comfortably. Above all,
they want a home where a child will feel wanted and loved.

An open adoption agreement is more likely to work if you
are dealing with adoptive parents who understand how much
this kind of arrangement can benefit the child.

Understanding the Legal Issues

If you make an adoption plan, you need to understand the legal matters. Adoption law varies greatly from state to state and province to province. Legal issues can seem difficult, and it's important to ask as many questions as it takes to understand thoroughly. Tatum commented:

I had questions about legal matters, and I got real confused. I didn't know the terms, and I asked Carolyn if she could explain it to me in a way I could understand.

She gave me a copy of the relinquishment papers, and each day we would go over it paragraph by paragraph. She would translate what it meant so I would understand it better.

Special Adoption Law for Native Americans

Adoption plans for Native American children must follow different rules. Before an American Indian child can be placed for adoption, the adoption facilitator must learn if that child is registered with his/her tribe. If so, the tribe has priority for the placement of that child. If the tribe is not contacted, they can come back at any time and take the child away from the adoptive parents.

If your child is of Native American descent and you are considering an adoption plan, it is important that you find out about these special laws. If you're planning an independent adoption, be sure the attorneys are carefully following the regulations. For more information, contact the Social Services of the tribal center or the American Indian Urban Center.

Costs of Adoption

If you make an independent adoption plan for your baby, the adoptive parents you choose are expected to pay the legal and other costs of the adoption. However, it is absolutely illegal for prospective adoptive parents to give the birthmother or birthfather a gift. Whatever she receives to pay medical bills and possibly her living expenses during pregnancy must be reported to the court. If you are ever approached by someone who wants to pay you to let them adopt your child, you should report that person to the authorities immediately!

Adoptive parents must file a statement when they adopt that they have paid only pregnancy costs and lawyer/agency fees. The law has always permitted this. If something more is added, it's illegal.

A criticism sometimes leveled at independent adoption is that, because the adoptive parents pay pregnancy-related expenses, the birthmother would have trouble changing her mind about the adoption. Even though in some states she doesn't sign the consent to adopt until several weeks, even months after delivery, she might find it difficult to back out of such an arrangement.

However, the birthmother has no legal obligation to pay back the expense money she received from the prospective adoptive family. According to law, she cannot release her child for adoption until after delivery. Money spent before delivery by the adoptive parents is spent in the hope and expectation of adopting that baby, but it is *not* dependent on the adoption being finalized.

If you decide to keep your baby, neither the adoptive parents nor their lawyer can legally require you to pay back the money spent on your medical and other pregnancy bills. Sometimes, if a young woman decides to keep her baby, she, her partner, or her parents will choose to repay the money spent on her pregnancy needs. They will not be required by law to do so, however.

Developing an adoption plan is one of the most important tasks you will ever face. After all, your baby's future hinges on that plan. *It's an awesome responsibility.*

CHAPTER 8

Selecting Your Baby's Family

We liked learning that adoption gave us some control. We set criteria for a family. Basically, we superimposed our interests and beliefs on a more mature set of parents. We wanted music in their background because Kathleen is an accomplished pianist. We wanted them involved in athletics because I am.

We wanted them to be older and more mature. We also wanted them to have a child already. We didn't care if it was adopted or biological, but we wanted them to have parenting experience. We chose a family with a strong Christian background. We chose a family moderately wealthy, upper middle class, because we wanted our child to be provided for.

The social worker brought us five letters from people she thought met our criteria. We read the letters separately, and we picked the same couple. We both knew they were the right parents for our child.

We met with them a couple of times. Although it was a little awkward for everybody, we knew this was who we wanted to parent our child.

Nick

I didn't choose a family for a long time. I had a hard time making that decision. I knew I wanted a black family because she is mixed with black. I wanted the mother and father to be married, and for them to have a big family that loved each other. And it all came together like little puzzle pieces, and I believe it was a miracle.

Jazmin

Selecting the Adoptive Parents

Responsible parents don't leave their child with strangers. If they need a babysitter, good parents will check that sitter out carefully before leaving their child with her, even if it's only for an hour or two.

How much more important it is that you choose carefully the people who will adopt your child! You expect these people to love and care for your child throughout his life. Even with an open adoption with continuing contact, you know that the adoptive parents will be the day-to-day parents.

As a birthparent, your love for your child will continue, but after the adoption is final, you will no longer have the right to make decisions for her. If you disagree with the way the adoptive parents interact with your child, you'll need to trust them and not interfere with their ways of parenting.

If your parents are already grandparents, they may have some similar feelings about their grandchildren. Your parents love their grandchildren dearly, but may not always agree with the way these children are being reared. At the same time, they know that the children's *parents* should be in control, not the grandparents.

And so it is with adoption. You will continue to love your child, but you will need to trust the adoptive parents on parenting issues.

Birthparents *are* ahead of grandparents in one sense. Birthparents, if they are involved in open adoption, will choose the mother *and* father for their child (assuming you want a two-parent family). Grandparents generally don't get to select their daughter- or son-in-law!

Falling in Love

So how do you make this all-important selection of adoptive parents for your child? Can you find a perfect family? No, probably not, just as most people don't find the perfect partner. We simply try to meet our needs in the best way we can. "Falling in love," of course, tends to be an important part of choosing our partner.

"Falling in love" is a term also used by some birthparents when they speak of choosing their child's adoptive parents:

My doctor told me about her two friends, Travis and Vanessa, who were in their late 30s. I read their resume and said I'd like to meet them. They flew down two days later. I spent the whole day with them and fell in love.

I asked them lots of personal questions, and I knew these were my baby's parents. From then on we wrote letters and talked on the phone. I sent them a sonogram.

Sonia

Although Erica first heard of her baby's family through a newspaper ad, a lot of research preceded her choice:

I contacted several agencies, but at that time (1991) there wasn't much choice. They had a lot of rules, and I didn't like them telling me what I had to do. They said they could give me a couple's phone number but I couldn't meet them. I felt they were acting only for the adoptive couples.

*When I started calling people in the USA **Today** ads, I liked some of them, but none was overwhelmingly right. Then I called Lena and Sam. We talked for a long time, and we seemed to have the same beliefs.*

Four days later I got a beautiful four-page letter from them which included lots of pictures. We talked a couple more times, then on my eighteenth birthday they came for a visit. From then on, it was Lena and Sam's baby. The visit was wonderful. After that, we sent them sonograms and called fairly often.

*My mom said, "You can't pick parents out of USA **Today**." Then we learned that in their state they had to be approved by Social Services **before** they got the baby. Then they have three visits the first year and two each year after that until the child is five. Sam and Lena even sent us a copy of their home study. That reassured us.*

If you consider selecting your child's adoptive parents from couples you first hear about through a newspaper ad, be extremely careful. Nancy Johnson, Spokane Consultants in Family Living, warns of the risks of choosing a couple in this way. You need to learn a lot about that couple before you trust them with your child.

"A young woman will find an ad in the paper, hook up with the couple on the phone, and they will tell her everything she wants to hear. That's not what adoption is about. It's not a quick fix," Johnson emphasized.

"The result may be a couple who rushes in at the time of labor, spends 48 hours in town, then whisks the baby away. That's when we have victimization of the birthparent. That's when the birthparents go into shock. Yet it's under the guise of open adoption," she said.

Full disclosure of identities is the rule with Spokane Consultants. "We make it clear to adoptive couples that that's an expectation," she said. "By the time the placement happens, this will be the way it is. If it's not, we want to know why. Adoptive parents need to be willing to reveal their lives before they adopt someone's child."

Building Trust with Adoptive Parents

Relationships need to be built on trust, and sometimes it's pretty hard to talk about trusting somebody you haven't met. If you make an effort to get to know the adoptive parents, you'll be building that important trust. A counselor/facilitator can help.

Enid Callen, The Adoption Connection, Highland Park, Illinois, explained, "In the beginning of the relationship, we can help facilitate meetings. As trust develops between the adoptive couple and the birthparents, we step out." That phrase, "As trust develops, we step out," is the goal you want your counselor/facilitator to have.

Should Family Resemble Yours?

What kind of parents would you like to have for yourself if you were choosing? Some birthparents are looking for an adoptive family similar to their own. They may get quite specific, as Nick and Kathleen did. Nick is quoted at the beginning of this chapter as saying they wanted a couple with interests and beliefs similar to their own, but a couple more mature than they were. They were delighted to find a couple who met these criteria.

Maggie's counselor helped Maggie develop criteria she would use in selecting adoptive parents for her child:

I met with Edna regularly, and we talked about what I was looking for. At about five months I went through files to pick the parents. I didn't want them to be smokers. I was looking for somebody who had religious beliefs but not overly so. I really wanted them to have another child. I grew up with an older brother, and this was important to me.

I didn't care if they were rich. As long as they could afford to have a child, that was fine with me. And I didn't want an older couple. I wanted somebody in their 30s.

So Edna gave me files of people who might match these things. I got real discouraged first time through because none of them were clicking, so I went back to Edna and she gave me three more. On the last one, the minute I opened it, it clicked. I knew these were the ones. Mark and Kathi are active people which I like because I'm active, too. Their letters were touching. They looked so happy, and so did their child, who also came to them through adoption. They were 42, a little older than I'd wanted, but I decided that was all right.

They were told of my decision, and they sent me a letter and some pictures. We made plans to meet with help from Edna. "What if they don't like me?" I asked.

"Put yourself in their place. If they don't like you, you can choose someone else, but they can't do the choosing," she said. So I realized I had the power.

They are real neat people. Kathi reminds me of my mom. They were very concerned about my feelings. We decided to meet again, this time with their son. That was good because I saw how they act with Riki. He was great. He was three, and the minute he saw me, he put his hand on my stomach and said, "That's my sister."

It made me happy, but also sad. It was bittersweet, but I knew I was doing a good thing. I was making Riki happy, I was making Mark and Kathi happy, and, most important, it was making my child happy.

If you choose a couple who are already parenting, spending time with them and their child can provide valuable information about their parenting skills. And if they are already involved with a birthfamily, it may be an indication of their willingness to continue a relationship with you after they have your child.

When Do You Choose a Family?

Most adoption counselors suggest that the ideal time to choose your child's adoptive family is six or seven months into your pregnancy. Your baby will be moving, and you may feel more "real" about your decision. Eleyna, however, chose her birthfamily when she was only three months pregnant. She was 14, felt she simply wasn't ready to parent, and thus had more time to build a relationship before she delivered:

> *I chose Park and Renee from the profiles Sarah showed me. I'm a dancer and Renee is a dancer, and I liked that. And I've lived in apartments all my life and couldn't have animals, and they have all these dogs and cats. I met them when I was three months along.*
>
> *During the rest of my pregnancy, we went out to movies and to eat, and we'd play games. They moved out of state a couple of months before I delivered, and I went up there once and saw their house. I liked knowing that was where my baby would live.*

Cerissa, who spent the last month of her pregnancy in the hospital, chose her child's adoptive parents from letters her counselor shared with her:

> *I wanted a mixed couple because the baby's father is Hispanic and I'm Caucasian. The mother I chose is Hispanic, and Ken is Caucasian. Maria owns a little Mexican restaurant. The letter was very down home. She wrote about a lot of relatives, and I wanted my child to have stacks of cousins.*
>
> *I read another letter from a family that seemed more qualified from a material standpoint. They had more money, two children, lots of education, but I liked how personable the letter was from Maria and Ken.*

Now, six years later, Cerissa has had recent contact with the family she selected. She feels she made a good choice.

It is risky, however, to choose your child's adoptive parents at the last minute. If you're making an adoption plan, you need to select the family well before your child is born so you have time to build a relationship with them before you trust them with your child. You don't, of course, make a final decision to release your child until *after* his birth.

Finding Right Parents Takes Time

David and Rita spent a great deal of time and effort in choosing the "right" family for their child. David commented:

> *Rita and I talked every day about the kind of family we wanted for our child. Money was not terribly important, but I wanted to make sure this child had two parents who were ready for a child. We wanted someone who couldn't have children biologically, and somebody who would make Christian values a big part of our child's life.*
>
> *We went through stacks of profiles, at least 20, and after awhile we started to narrow it down. It bothered me that most people write letters only to the birth-**mothers** without anything about the birthfather. Many of the letters seemed to follow a pattern — they all appeared to be saying the same thing.*
>
> *We would look at the profiles separately, then talk about them. We agreed immediately on the couple we chose. Their letter was different than the others. Both John and Glenda wrote, and they really wanted a child. The letters were heart-felt and emotional. I could tell these people were hurting. They wanted a child, and they were ready for that child.*
>
> *We met them, and it was amazing. When we walked out, we each said, "I knew they were right the minute we walked in." They were young and vibrant, and much like us. All four of us sat in that room for two hours, and we all cried. Their three-year wait might finally be coming*

*to an end. We saw them again a few days later, and
that's when we told them they were the ones for us.*

Alexis worked with a counselor, but she also wanted her
mother involved:

*My mom went with me for the second meeting with
the adoptive parents. I think that's important. Otherwise,
unless you're with the father, it's two versus one because
the counselor is supposed to be the mediator.*

*Sometimes the birthmom doesn't know what her
rights are, and the fact that the adoptive parents are
dishing out the money may give them an advantage.*

Building a Relationship

Some birthparents select their adoptive couple by reading
resumes. Others select several, then interview them personally
before making a final decision. Whichever approach you
follow, you probably want to see them several times before
you deliver. In this way, you're more likely to build a strong
and lasting relationship. Alexis explained the reassurance she
received from seeing Troy and Cynthia several times:

*They live six hours away, and they came down a
couple of times, and then my mom and I visited them.
Then they came down again during my final month.*

*That last month visit was important because I was
getting bad feelings about losing my baby. I loved them,
but I was hating them because they were going to be
able to parent my child and I wasn't. The reality was
coming closer.*

*But when we could talk in person, they were still
"them," and not the evil people that were coming into
my thoughts. They said later they were having some of
the same feelings.*

Kernisha talked about building a relationship with the
adoptive family:

I was only five months pregnant when I went to the agency. I already knew I would place for adoption, and I was ready to look at profiles. I wanted to meet the parents as soon as possible because I wanted to build a strong relationship with them before he was born.

We had two days together the first time they flew up to meet me, and then we talked by phone every week until I delivered in March.

My hospital time wasn't easy, but I was prepared. I started my mourning before Scotty was born. I was sure of my decision, and by then I loved Tony and Darlene.

Scotty is three months old now, and I still talk with them every week. They're bringing him up in July for my birthday. They send me pictures and I have their address. We don't have anything to hide. The more I see Tony and Darlene, the more secure I feel. They have framed pictures of me in their house because I'm a big part of their life.

If I were placing again and the family didn't want openness, I'd look for another family. Having a relationship with Tony and Darlene makes the adoption better. It will also help our son grow up well-rounded with all these people loving him.

I had to build a relationship with them because if I didn't know them, I wasn't going to place with them. And I never changed my mind. I didn't go back and forth with my decision. You do have a sense of power, and it's your responsibility to know what you want, and that you don't play games with the adoptive parents you choose.

I feel if we had waited to build our relationship and I'd not been as close when he was born, I wouldn't have this comfort inside when I placed him.

Kernisha

You would be wise to have an idea of the amount of openness you want *before* you select adoptive parents. If you "click" on a couple, meet them, and like them, you might be willing to give up too much to please them. You want to be true to your wishes for an open relationship with your child's adoptive family.

You're more likely to be able to maintain an open relationship if the family lives reasonably close to you rather than across the country—although you or they may move later.

Choosing Parents in Special-Needs Adoption

La Tasha had not yet made an adoption plan when her twins were born three months early. In fact, her family was strongly opposed to adoption:

> *I was considering adoption before I delivered, but my family was against it. When I had twins, I knew in my heart I couldn't take care of them. They weighed two pounds each, and had to stay in the hospital for three months.*
>
> *A speaker at school made a difference. She talked about adoption, and afterward I asked her questions. She knew I must be pregnant. I gave her my phone number and she called and we talked.*
>
> La Tasha

Generally, birthparents of infants have a wide choice of adoptive parents. They may choose a family from a group of resumes, then interview that family and perhaps others before making a decision. La Tasha, with two special-needs babies, did not have as wide a choice as most of the others. However, she, too, found an adoptive couple eager to love and care for her tiny twins:

> *The first couple I picked didn't want my kids. They were worried because the babies were so tiny and had to stay in the hospital for three months.*
>
> *Then the lawyer gave me another profile. I read it*

and thought, "These are the people I want for my kids."
I met the couple, and we went to the hospital to meet the
babies. They were ecstatic when they saw the twins.

I told them flat out, "These are going to be your
children. You need to get close to them and they need to
get close to you." We were together a lot the last two
months the babies were in the hospital.

La Tasha was deeply hurt when the first couple said they
didn't want her babies because of their special needs. She
might have avoided this hurt if she had gone to an adoption
agency instead of to an attorney.

Working with an adoption agency is usually the best
approach to making an adoption plan for a child with special
needs. Agencies are likely to have more experience and to
have a wide bank of potential adoptive parents waiting,
including some who are interested in special-needs children.

Choosing Family for Third Child

Aryanna already had two children and had finally managed
to get off public aid when she realized she was pregnant
again. She says the day she found out about the pregnancy she
knew she had to make an adoption plan.

The first day I cried all day and I cried all night.
Then I called an agency here in town. They were very
professional, very nice and well-mannered, but very
business-like. It was just a procedure for them, not very
personal. That wasn't what I needed.

I was upset, but I knew I would do what was best for
this little child. I was hoping to find a warm kind of
kinship with the people I would be working with. I found
that in Adoption Connection. They were sweet and so
supportive of me as a person.

I was 27 when Ryan was born. I didn't feel judged at
all because they were so warm and caring.

I first talked with Enid when I was about two months pregnant. Shortly after that I took my youngest son to see her. I shared my story, and told her what I was looking for. I wanted a couple who had been married for awhile, who believed in God, and I hoped to find a mom who was a stay-at-home, at least for the first couple of years. I wanted a couple who enjoy life, and I hoped they would share photos and letters with me. I wanted them to tell my child about the adoption early in his life.

The couple I chose already had an adopted son who was five, and they were involved in support groups for adoptive parents. They're everything I wanted.

I met their little boy a couple of times before my baby was born. They were honest and warm and very open. I can see how the adoptive couple could be concerned, wondering if the birthmother might change her mind. And the birthmom is afraid of losing the connection with them, of being forgotten by the family.

We all want what's best for the little one, and we don't want to do anything to disrupt his life. When people ask me if I worry about his well-being, I tell them I talked with the adoptive couple at length. I had my preferences, and if we hadn't agreed, we could each have looked further. I made a good choice.

Whatever your situation, if you select your child's adoptive parents carefully, and if you are very open with them about yourself, and especially about your dreams for your child, they are likely to be open with you. The relationship you form with each other will be important to your child.

You have not only a right, but also a responsibility to be as sure as you can possibly be that the couple receiving your baby are the kind of people you want to parent your child. Finding out as much as you can about these people is important. Feeling positive and loving toward them is crucial.

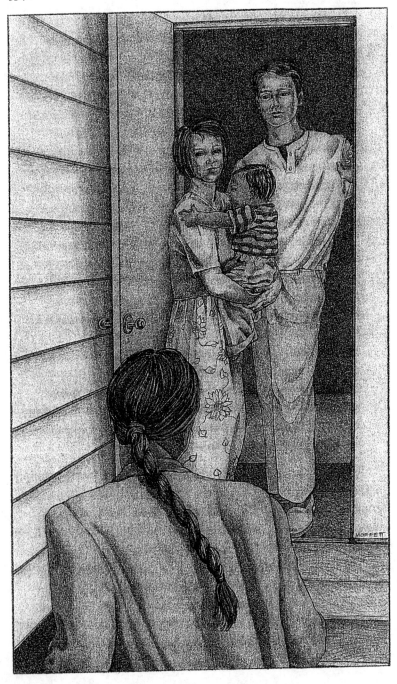

CHAPTER 9

How Much Contact Between Families?

I wanted a completely open adoption, and they only had two families willing to be that open. I clicked on one. They looked like the right place for my baby to grow up. They have a nice house with a big back yard. Her dad likes to go fishing.

It's completely open. I have their address, and we write back and forth and don't go through the agency. I talk with them directly, and it's really great.

Carmen

Is Separation of Families Advisable?

Sometimes people suggest that the fact of adoption means there "should" be a separation between the adoptive and birthfamilies. They say it's not appropriate for the two families to form a close relationship.

Leaders in open adoption disagree. "The emotional

distance these adoptive parents describe is a matter of choice, not necessity," Melina and Roszia state in *The Open Adoption Experience* (page 196). They point out that many adoptive parents develop a friendship that includes the birthparents babysitting or going on vacation with the family. They don't find this confuses the child or makes it harder for them to form an attachment to or effectively parent the child.

Discussing Amount of Openness

You need to be very clear about the contact you want with the adoptive parents you choose. At the same time, realize you may want to change the guidelines as the years go by. Talking to the adoptive parents about this possibility is wise. Recently birthparents and adoptive parents tend to have more and more contact, with some developing close relationships.

Sarah Jensen, Adoption Center of San Diego, tells birthparents, "Be prepared that what you think you want now in openness will probably increase over time. Some birthparents call and say. 'I'll want pictures but I won't want visits.'

"I call them and say, 'Why not? Once you know these people you may feel more comfortable about contact with them.'" Jensen stresses that the birthparents and the adoptive parents need to develop a fluid relationship that can change.

When a birthparent tells Jensen she doesn't want contact with the adoptive parents, Jensen responds, "You can't really make that decision until you meet them. You may find you really want a lot of contact with them."

If either the birthparents or the adoptive parents say they don't want contact with the other, what is this saying to your child? Your child needs to know you are a good person. Both you and the adoptive parents need to help him understand that, while you are giving him another family, you still care about him.

Birthparents need to realize that the reason adoptive couples are committed to openness is usually because they think it's best for the child. "If you think it would be too painful for you to spend time with them, will you write your child a letter? Will you send pictures of you and the birthfather?" Jensen asks.

"Adoptees need to know that birthmom is never going to forget them," she continued. "If she disappears, the adoptee may think he's forgotten. The birthparent has a right to disappear if it's too painful, but she needs to leave at least a letter for her child."

If this is how you feel—that you think getting involved with your baby and the adoptive parents is not what you want—you might at least acknowledge the possibility that you could change your mind later.

Perhaps the adoptive parents will send letters and pictures to the agency, independent adoption center, or attorney who arranged the adoption. When/If you wish to see them, they will be available. You also need to stay in touch with your facilitator so that your child can contact you when she's ready.

How Much Contact?

Potential adoptive parents who work with Jensen are educated on the advantages of open adoption. "People say, 'Should I give her (birthmother) my address?'" Jensen said.

"I say, 'Well, she's giving you her baby. It seems fair that you give her your address.'"

Some agencies offer a model agreement for contact between birth and adoptive parents. For example, the adoptive families at one agency are expected to send pictures and letters six times the first year, then annually for 18 years. Some recommend that contact be through the agency unless the adoptive parents and the birthparents agree to exchange full names and addresses in order to correspond with, and perhaps visit each other. Over time, direct contact between families is likely to work best.

Deborah Crouse Cobb, adoption attorney, tells potential

adoptive families that if they don't keep their promises to the
birthparents, she will never work with them again. "I haven't
had much problem with that," she commented. "If you educate adoptive families, it's rare for them to back out.

"I tell adoptive families things that blow their minds. They
sit in my office and say, 'I could never do this (place a baby
for adoption).'

"I tell them if they mean that, they have no business
adopting because if that would be best for their child, they
need to be able to do it. If they can't do what's best for the
child, they have no business parenting.

"I tell them to think about what they would do if they were
finding a family for their child, put themselves in the
birthparents' shoes. I make couples think about this concept.
When you learn not to be selfish and you value your child's
birthparents, you won't renege on your promises."

Occasionally birthmothers have called Cobb to report they
haven't gotten the promised pictures. "I call the adoptive
parents and say, 'She hasn't gotten any pictures.'

"'Oh, we forgot. We'll get them right out,' and they do. I'm
real clear—you don't make promises you can't keep. I haven't
had problems. Actually I have four or five files where the
adopting couples have followed through on their agreements
but the birthmothers are not interested in keeping in touch at
this time. The pictures and letters go into a file here until she
says she wants to be in contact with them again."

Adoptive parents and birthparents may want openness at
different times. The adoptive parents might prefer to spend the
first weeks, perhaps months, bonding with the baby. It is
during this time that the birthparents are likely to be grieving
and especially need contact with the adoptive family. Later,
when the birthparents may be focusing on other aspects of
their lives, the adoptive parents may want more contact. If
each is sensitive to the others' needs, and if the focus is on the
child, satisfying contact is more likely to continue.

Two Adoptions—One Closed, One Open

Emily has placed two children for adoption. For each, she chose the family carefully, and she knew she wanted to continue contact with her children's families. Her relationship with the two families is very different, and she explains some possible reasons for those differences.

For my first baby, I went to an attorney. He had hundreds of profiles of people who wanted to adopt a child. I read six and selected one.

I wanted to meet the family, but they didn't want a face-to-face meeting. Instead, they called me and we talked a long time. I thought I knew a lot about them.

I gave birth, they adopted my baby, and I heard from them a couple of times after that. Then at five months, they cut off all contact. Now it's a closed adoption. I was hurt, because I think it should be a trusting relationship. I gave them the most precious gift possible, and they don't trust me.

He's four now. I continue to write letters. They don't, but I do. If we're reunited, I have my life in those letters.

If the family you select doesn't want to meet you, you may want to make another selection. Why wouldn't they want to meet their child's birthparent? It's usually hard to build a relationship without trust.

More Openness This Time

Emily continued her story:

When I got pregnant again, I still wasn't ready to parent. I knew I would insist on pictures and letters, and I knew I had to meet this family face to face. I contacted an agency this time, and I chose Sheila and Norbert. We met, and when they first mentioned open adoption, I had no clue as to what it meant. I had heard of birth-

*mothers who got to see their children once or twice a
year, but this is much more open.*

*We met that first night and they said, "Here's our
address. Here's our phone number." You can say anything on the phone, but when we met face to face and
looked each other in the eye, I knew they were more
likely to do what they promised.*

*Louita is 19 months old now, and I have babysat for
them three times, she and her sister, who is their biological daughter. They call me when they're in a jam. It's
nice because it gives me time to spend with Louita and
learn her habits. We have a nice time together, and it
makes me realize I made the right choice this time.*

Sometimes Communication Stops

Adoptive parents, of course, are unique just as birthparents
are. And in most states, birthparents have no legal recourse if
the adoptive parents stop communication with them after the
adoption is final. Cecelia shared the pain of losing contact
with her child and the adoptive family. It can happen.

*I really liked the fact that I got to pick the adoptive
parents, I got to meet them, I got to know them. I didn't
think I could go through a closed adoption because I
would worry about my child.*

*The first couple I chose got another baby before I
delivered. Then I chose Roger and Lucille. They had
gotten close to a birthmother, and she changed her mind
the second day after she delivered. That was real hard
on them.*

*I could tell they were a little hesitant to get close, but
I figured I could understand that because of what they
had gone through. They agreed to pictures every year
and said I could see my daughter when she was two. I
thought that would be okay.*

I met them a couple more times before Ruth was born.

I saw them in the hospital, and when I signed papers.

I didn't get any pictures the first month and I was kind of upset so I called Adoption Connection. Roger and Lucille sent some photos. Then I didn't get any more for quite awhile so I wrote to them. I finally got pictures— the same pictures!

They have my daughter and I don't want to think meanly of them. Time went on and I hadn't gotten my next set of photos. I wrote them a letter and told them I was feeling bad, and that it would be nice if they would send the pictures they had promised me. I finally got more pictures, but they were several months old.

They completely stopped sending pictures when Ruth was one. So Adoption Connection set up a meeting for me with the father in a park. I asked for pictures four times a year but he said that was too often. He agreed to once a year. I got photos a year later, but that's the last time I heard from them. That was two years ago.

I have their name and address although they don't think I do. They told The Adoption Connection that they had fulfilled their obligation at one year, and they don't need to do any more.

After I heard that, I wrote them a letter, and I have to say it was the meanest letter I have ever written— although it wasn't a mean letter. I just have so much frustration toward them. At the same time I want to love them because they are parenting my daughter. I don't like conflict, and I always weigh both sides, but this time I think I'm getting the bad deal. Where I am is standing in a courtroom with her holding my finger, and you have her the rest of her life. I told them I felt they lied to me in order to get my daughter—say whatever you can and run with her, although I wasn't that blunt.

I wish I had had more communication with them at the start. I think if we had known each other better, they

*might have understood I wouldn't be a problem. I think
they wanted to make the best impression they could, and
they weren't honest. I'd have been much better off with
honesty at the time instead of a whole lot of hurt later.*

*I've learned that Roger and Lucille did not attend the
adoptive parent seminars. That might have made a
difference in their trust toward me. For open adoption to
work, the adoptive parents have to understand what
open adoption is, and that the birthmother will be part
of their lives.*

If it is a legitimate relationship, there should be no reason
for it to stop. What is important is that everyone be comfortable with the relationship, and that you all realize that relationships do change over time. You need to be able to talk
about these changes together. Having an intermediary can
help in a situation like this.

You probably want to become as close to the adoptive
parents as you can before your child is born. They need to
understand that having them rear your child is your wish, and
at the same time, you need to know they will not drop out of
your life as soon as they have your baby. You all need to
remember your child is the real winner in open adoption.

Cecelia occasionally participates in panel discussions with
birthparents. After hearing about her lack of contact with the
adoptive family, many of the adoptive parents come to her and
say, "I can't get the birthmother to write back. I send her
pictures and I don't get anything back." A break-down in
communication will hurt, whether it's the adoptive parents or
the birthparents who close the door.

Enforcing Open Adoption Agreement

In a few states, including Washington, an open adoption
agreement between the birthparents and adoptive parents can
be submitted to the court at the time of relinquishment. This is
considered enforceable, and can be taken to the local court for

help in enforcing it, according to Nancy Johnson, Spokane, Washington. "It doesn't mean the child will be returned to the birthparents," she pointed out. However, adoptive parents are not likely to want to force court involvement in their open adoption agreement. Three visits or contacts annually between birth and adoptive parents is a typical agreement in their organization, Johnson said.

Johnson pointed out that it is important for the birthparents to see the adoptive parents and the child as a family. The contact agreement is not a one-on-one relationship of the birthparent and the child. The birthparent does not have the parenting role.

What is your role as a birthparent? It might be compared to a favorite aunt, or a loved friend of the family. In some adoptive families, the birthmother occasionally babysits. Others don't think this is appropriate because they feel babysitting is too much like parenting. Johnson mentioned a birthmother who wanted to babysit, but the adoptive mother didn't agree because she felt the time the birthmother spent with the child should be a pleasure time without the added responsibility of babysitting.

You may find that you and the adoptive parents will not become close even though you make your selection very carefully. It's a little like in-laws. You may not feel close to them, but you give them respect because of their role in your family. So it may be with adoptive and birthfamilies.

Always remember that you can help the communication along. You may not like to write letters, for example, but if you discipline yourself to do your share of the corresponding, your child's adoptive parents are more likely to keep in touch with you.

The beauty of open adoption is that *you* and your child's adoptive parents make these decisions. There are no rules to follow—except the big rule of everyone doing their best to figure out what's best for this child you *all* love.

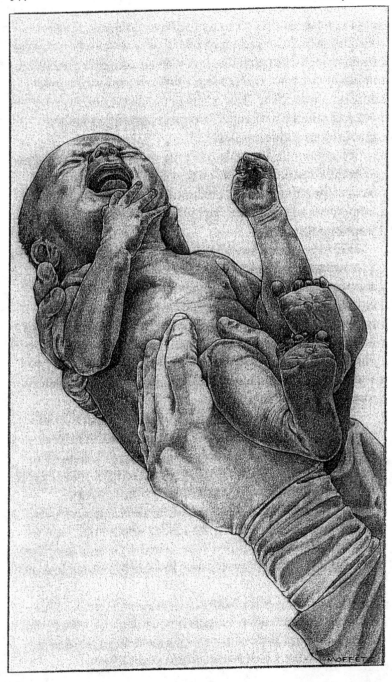

CHAPTER 10

Your Baby Is Born

After I had him, it was the most amazing thing—the biggest miracle on the face of this planet. James even smelled great. He grabbed my finger, and I thought, "This is the purest form of love there is."

They took him to the nursery while I was in recovery. My mom was there, and some friends brought me flowers.

I never had anyone saying to me, "Why are you placing your baby?" We were all bonding with each other. I stayed in the hospital for three days, and I spent every waking moment with James. I slept for five days after I went home because I was exhausted.

We spent all this time looking at each other. My pastor came in and we had a little blessing for him down in the chapel.

Lisette

*I watched my son come into the world. When
Cameron came out, I cut the umbilical cord. When he
opened his eyes, mine was the first face he saw. As I held
him in my arms, something inside my heart just broke.*

*I held him for a few minutes, then wrapped him up,
and handed him to Rita.*

*John and Glenda were waiting outside the door. I
took him out and put him in their arms.*

*That's the most difficult thing I have ever done in my
life. I had to lay aside my pride and know that I couldn't
take care of him.*

David

Your Baby Is Finally Here

For some mothers, childbirth is a difficult, long task. For
others, it happens quickly and fairly easily. Being prepared
helps. Taking a childbirth education class and doing your
prepared childbirth exercises can help with the physical
process.

Childbirth, whether difficult or relatively easy, is followed
by the usually joyful event of the mother finally having her
baby in her arms. For a birthmother, it is a bittersweet joy. She
knows if she carries out her adoption plan, she will be with
her baby for only a brief time before placement.

*The day Jenae was born was the happiest day of my
life. I stayed in the hospital three days because you have
to wait 72 hours to sign adoption papers. I didn't want
to go home, and I didn't want her in foster care.*

*I slept only twelve hours in four days because I
wanted to be with her every single minute. Nick slept in
the room on the floor each night. The last night we sat
there with Jenae the whole night and talked and cried.
We talked about everything we were going to miss in her
life. We talked about how she looked like Nick, and
about her and her life without us. I think it was one of*

the most healing things that could have happened. We
were grieving together, the three of us.

Kathleen

For most birthparents, this time with the baby is compli-
cated by the fact that the adoption versus parenting decision
may have to be made all over again. Finally your baby is here,
in your arms. Carrying out your adoption plan is likely to be
harder than you expected.

I expected to stay in the hospital only one day, but my
blood pressure shot way up and I had to stay three days.
That must have been planned so I could spend those
three days with Rosie while I healed. I spent a lot of time
crying. I would sit there and look at her and cry. Some
of my closest family members came in and held her.
Rosie spent very little time in the nursery.

I would hold her, she would give a little smirk, and I
would think, "Do I really want to do this?" I think that's
what made me bond. Of course we bonded during the
whole nine months, but being able to have those three
days with her, caring for her as a mother, I will never
forget that.

When they finally took Rosie — my brother was
sitting beside me when they came in with the papers. I
was hesitant — can I stay a couple more days? But I
signed the papers.

Yvette

Decision Remade After Birth

No matter how firm your were in your adoption decision,
you remake that decision after you give birth. "Every bit of
reason goes out the window when you pick up that newborn,"
a counselor commented.

To some extent, you can prepare for this time. If you
haven't had much experience with new babies, go to the

hospital and see the babies while you're still pregnant. Know that your baby will be absolutely beautiful. You will be proud of your baby, and you will wonder how you can possibly part with him/her.

For a long time, birthmothers were told they shouldn't see their babies after delivery. This wasn't a healthy plan. Birthparents need to say "Hello" before they say "Goodbye."

> *I told the doctor I didn't want to hold Joshua, and I didn't want to see him. But I saw him and I said, "I have to hold him." I had him for nine months, and I had a feeling of dread and a feeling of happiness, so many mixed emotions.*
>
> *I didn't make the decision again. I knew I was going to be giving him up. I knew these were the last days I would have with him, and I wanted to make the most of them.*
>
> Sonia

If at all possible, you need to feel okay about your adoption plan before you go into delivery. "Your heart takes over during delivery," a young woman commented.

Wendy Heiser, Bethany Christian Services, Seattle, Washington, talked about preparing for this time. "Before delivery we brainstorm the good things and the bad things about placing. I tell her that when she goes to the hospital she will have a lot of hormones going, she will be hurting a lot.

"We talk about head decisions versus heart decisions. We warn them, 'Your heart is going to be very strong when you look at that little baby. Your heart is going to want to override your head. It is important you distinguish between your head and your heart.' They are going to be faced with hospital workers coming in and saying, 'Is this what you really want?' Sometimes we bring out that list we worked on before . . . 'Remember, you said you want to go on to school, you don't want to be on welfare, you want more for your baby.'

"We look back on what we have worked on, the things we've covered. It's important that the birthmom knows it is safe to talk. The birthmom may feel real guilty if she should change her mind. She needs to know it is her decision. She can place the baby in foster care temporarily if she needs to. She can ask for more time after the baby is born," Heiser concluded.

Write Your Reasons

While you're still pregnant, write down the reasons you're making an adoption plan. Put those reasons in the bag you take to the hospital. After your child is born, get out your list.

Other people will probably be giving you lots of advice, but your own thinking is most important as you make your final decision. The reasons you were planning adoption are probably still there. At least you can balance them with the feelings you encounter as you spend time with your baby.

I walked around in labor for a day, but I wasn't sure it was the real thing. We got to the hospital when the contractions were about three minutes apart. Then came the complications. I had a stubborn little girl who would not crown. We did everything we could to get her to turn around when they said she was breech. I was like, this kid is going to be me all over again with her stubbornness.

They were ready to consider a C-section when she suddenly pushed right out, and she was so pretty. I spent three days with her, and that last day we were back at the trying-to-make-a-decision stage. I called my mom and I said, "Mom, I don't know what to do."

My mom said, "Whatever you decide to do, I'll stand behind you. If you decide to bring her home, we'll manage."

I sat there for about an hour and kept asking myself,

"What can I give this child?"

Now I grew up in a single-parent family, and I asked myself if I wanted the same thing for my child. I decided I wanted more for her. My mom was a good mother, but there were times when we needed a father. I didn't want that for my daughter.

So I decided to sign the papers. She was there with me when I signed. After that I held her and played with her for about three hours, and then I went home. I felt in my heart I was doing the right thing. It was a challenge, but I don't have any regrets.

Tatum

Adoptive Parents' Involvement

How much do you want the adoptive parents involved in your baby's birth and during your hospital stay? Sometimes the adoptive parents take the birthmother to prepared childbirth classes and plan to be her coach during labor and delivery. This is a fine plan if *you* want them to be this involved. Maggie didn't ask the adoptive parents to be her coach, but she had hoped they could witness her/their baby's birth:

I paged Mark and Kathi when I went into the hospital, but Jessica was born before they got there. I wish they had made it. That would have been neat, especially for Kathi. We had talked about it, but I had such a fast labor, it didn't work out. It was important to tell them I would have liked them to be there.

I never had any doubts about placing her. It was hard for me, but I never had any doubts. Mark and Kathi were with me in the hospital for the three days I stayed.

I hadn't decided how much contact I would want with Jessica in the hospital. When she was born, I knew I wanted her with me the whole time. My friends said, "Are you sure? That's going to make it harder." To me, it's a very personal thing, very individual, and I knew it would be the best thing for me to get to know her those three days, to spend time with her, and to be able to look back on those days and remember.

Mark and Kathi were very respectful of my time. They were clear about not wanting to intrude.

Rita has some regrets, although not about placing Cameron with the family she and David chose. Rather, she thinks she could have handled the situation better if she had had more physical contact with their baby. She recalled:

The only thing I regret was that when he was born I didn't really get to see the baby. David took Cameron out so fast that I barely got to hold him. I didn't get to look in his eyes. He took him out to John and Glenda as soon as they cleaned him up.

John and Glenda stayed for that day and I was kind of there by myself. I got to hold him a couple of times, and I regret that I didn't get any pictures of me holding him.

Every time I asked to see him, I only got him for a couple of minutes. I found out later that it was the adoptive parents that wanted him back so they could feed him.

I don't really blame them, but I only got to see him twice, hold him for five or ten minutes. They were afraid I would change my mind. It hurt me then because every time I would start to look at him, they would come in and say it's time for his feeding.

After the parents had gone home that night, I heard a knock on the door. It was a night shift nurse and she had the baby. She said, "I just had to bring him by and show you."

He had his whole fist in his mouth, and I think that was the last time I got to see him. I never got to walk down to the nursery and see the babies in their little cribs. I went home the next day and that ended it.

I cried a lot when I left the hospital, but within a day or two we were back to our normal lives. Within a month I got a job and I was really okay with it.

They sent us pictures right away, within about three weeks, and two or three months later we met the parents for dinner. They brought an album of pictures, and that helped a lot.

Rita

This Is Your Time

It's important that you and the adoptive parents talk about their possible involvement during and immediately after your child's birth. You all need to realize that you may feel differently after delivery about the time you have with your baby.

If your one or two, possibly three days in the hospital will be the only time you parent this child, you may want to have much of the time alone with him/her. The adoptive parents need to realize this is your time. The amount of time they spend with the baby is up to you.

Before I went into labor, I wrote a letter about what I wanted to do after she was born.

I was in the hospital four days, and Troy and Cynthia stayed in a hotel nearby. I slept the entire day after delivery, and they spent that day with Betsy. I was with her a lot the next two days. In fact, I sent Troy and Cynthia out of the room the second day, and Troy was very upset. He told me later that they felt left out.

I wasn't prepared for how hard it would be after those two days with her. I told Troy and Cynthia to come at 11 the last day because I was to be released at 12. I got off the phone and bawled. That was the first time I lost it.

They came in at 10 instead of 11, but I said, "No, come at 11. Don't make this harder than it has to be."

They came back at 11 and I gave Betsy to them, and it

was real hard. She started to cry, and I stayed away so Cynthia would know that it was her turn. She comforted Betsy so differently than I had been doing. I started to cry again.

We left a few minutes later.

Alexis

You may find your time in the hospital is a time of bonding not only with your baby, but also with the adoptive parents.

After Scotty was born, we hung around and kept an eye on him while her family was with Kernisha. Then when he was ready, they let us carry Scotty down to her. We handed him to Kernisha. "I want you to know now that Scotty is born, I still feel the same way," she said.

When she said she wanted those 48 hours with him in the hospital, it scared me. But Wendy (counselor) assured me this was her time to say good-bye.

That last day she got real emotional. She cried a lot and I cried a lot. I don't think she saw me crying because I'd leave the room or go to the bathroom. I didn't want people to see me crying.

During that time we became close to Kernisha's parents and her grandparents. That's when we really bonded.

Darlene, adoptive mother

Dealing with Hospital Staff

You will probably have caring and helpful nurses much of the time in the hospital. Many women talk about the wonderful support they received from nurses while they were in labor, in the delivery room, and afterward. You may find, however, that not all nurses understand how to be supportive of an adoption plan.

First of all, no nurse should presume to know what your final decision will be, and no nurse should try to influence that decision:

A nurse saw me holding and feeding Eddie. When his parents came in, the nurse told them she thought I would keep him which devastated the adoptive parents. That happens a lot—nurses saying things like that.

People don't encourage a person to release her baby, and I think it's so wrong for people to interfere. I had no intention of keeping him. I was very committed to my plan. It hurt a lot, but I was still committed.

Maya

Alvera's doctor didn't think she should place her baby for adoption, and he was quite vocal about it. He barely made it to the hospital to assist with the delivery. Then Alvera had to cope with uncooperative hospital staff:

The hospital wasn't all that bad until they found out I wasn't parenting. I asked to be moved from the babies' floor to a regular medical floor. I had researched adoption, and I knew it would be hard on me to be on that floor with those babies. I knew your emotions can take over after delivery and you can do crazy things like taking him home.

The hospital moved me reluctantly. I wanted to get up and leave but they wouldn't let me. It was real hard. I went to see him in the nursery but they never brought him to my room. I fell in love with him. I knew I was doing something special for him and something special for his adoptive family.

People don't realize you have all these rights that any mother has until you actually sign the adoption papers.

Alvera, of course, is right. Until you sign the adoption papers, you have the same rights any mother has. If someone at the hospital should suggest you don't, that you shouldn't spend time with your baby, for example, be sure you assert your right to parent your child as much as you wish during this time.

Too Many Questions Asked

Derek and Danielle were bothered by the thoughtless comments several nurses made:

Probably the most upsetting things that happened during those nine months were the nurses' comments. Six or eight of them said, "It will be so nice to get your baby home," and we had been clear going in that we had an adoption plan. The nurses seemed to be totally ignorant of what was going on.

Derek

After Damon was born, every nurse on every shift had to know the whole story. We had to explain ourselves five or six times. Some of them didn't even know we were placing him.

For Derek and me, this was the only time we could parent, the only time we could be a family. Having nurses coming in asking these things made it difficult. We didn't want to talk about it. We asked a nurse to put a note on our door saying what we were doing so we wouldn't have to explain it over and over, but that didn't help much.

*To top all that, we wanted to be out of there by noon. At 11:45 I was feeding the baby and saying good-bye to him when a nurse came in and plopped down on the bed. "Have you **really** thought about this? Are you sure you want to do this?" That damaged the time that should have been special for us.*

Perhaps talking with the director of nursing would help. Derek got pretty angry. I tend to roll with these things. I told myself they don't know, they don't know what they're doing.

Danielle

Your hospital time is likely to be more satisfying if you talk with hospital personnel ahead of time. Write down your plans

Sample Birth Plan

Name_____ **Date**_____

    I plan to deliver my baby in _____ Hospital, and my due date is _____. I have made an open adoption plan for my baby. I have chosen _____ and _____ _____ to be his/her adoptive parents.

My adoption counselor _____

Attorney _____

Hospital contact_____

Labor Specifics:

My coach's name_____

Others I would like with me in labor and/or delivery:

Delivery:

I have attended childbirth preparation classes with my coach, but please help us if needed.

I want to know the baby's status immediately.

I wish to see my baby in recovery.

Postpartum:

I will have the baby in my room upon request. He can be shown to relatives and to the adoptive parents when they are with me.

If my baby is a boy, he is to be circumcised before being discharged from the hospital.

I understand that I may change my mind about the above details, or even the adoption plan, while I am in the hospital.

Please send baby pictures and memorabilia to me at the following address: _____

_____

_____

Signature

for the birth. (See page 156 for a sample plan.) When do you want the adoptive parents to be there? Do you want your baby with you? Then send copies of your hospital plan to your doctor, the director of nursing, hospital social worker, and anyone else who might be involved. Also pack a copy in your bag to take with you to the hospital.

Your Time Together

While you're in the hospital is a good time to write a letter to your baby in which you explain why you're giving him an adoptive family. Ask the adoptive parents to save your letter for your child to read in a few years. Even if you are forming a close relationship with the adoptive family, and will continue seeing your child, a letter written at this time will be treasured by your child. If you don't stay in contact, it will be reassuring when he wonders why you didn't rear him yourself.

Your time in the hospital with your baby will be a time you will always remember. It's a special time when you are the parent, although you may choose to share this role with the adoptive parents.

If you carry out your adoption plan, the interval with your baby will be over when you place him with his adoptive parents. You'll want to make the most of the time you have.

CHAPTER 11

Time to
Say Good-Bye

*When I left the hospital, Mark and Kathi brought me
a gift and a card and a sample of the wallpaper that
would be the border in Jessica's room. They gave me a
necklace that was really special, and that was when I
started to cry. I needed to let it out, and somehow I felt
okay crying in front of them.*

*We decided I would have my last time with Jessica in
the hospital room. Then I would call the nurse, she
would take Jessica, and I would leave the hospital. Then
they would take her. I held her and cried, and felt better
doing that, getting my sadness out.*

*I felt very lonely leaving the hospital. I had been
sleeping with Jessica for nine months, and that first
night alone in my room was really hard, awful.*

Maggie

Lucille and Roger got there a couple of hours after I delivered. I had warned them I would have a bunch of friends visiting me, and I did. They spent most of their time down at the window looking at Ruth.

The next day I was having a hard time, and I called them and asked them to wait a day so she could stay with me. I was freaking out, and when I asked them not to come, Roger was upset.

When I left the next day, everyone knew I was placing, but we were acting as if I wasn't. Ruth went home with them, and the court appearance was two days later. I said I wanted to spend a few minutes alone with her, and they agreed. I told her I hoped I'd see her later, and how much I loved her.

Cecelia

Planning a Placement Ceremony

A placement ceremony can help you celebrate the birth of your child even as you release her to her adoptive parents. Some birthparents choose not to participate in the placement ceremony because they are concerned that their grief will mar the joy of the adoptive parents receiving the baby. However, you may find that the ceremony will actually help you heal.

I took Archie home with me the day after I delivered. I spent the day with him, and then the adoptive parents came over. We had a celebration service.

It was like a party. Karen (counselor) *read some things from the Bible. Then everyone talked about how they had known me, and that this was God's decision. We had cookies and punch, and we both thanked each other. I gave Archie a plaque with an angel, "Lord, watch over this child," and they put it in his room. Renee gave me a "day of beauty," massage, etc.*

They send me pictures, we talk on the phone. They called me on Mother's Day and I liked that. I'm making a photo album for Archie with pictures of me when I was pregnant and when I was a little girl, and pictures of his birthfather.

Eleyna

Some birthparents are so committed to their decision and feel so close to the adoptive family that they are ready to be included in the presentation ceremony soon after birth. If not, an entrustment ceremony may be held at a later time.

Helpful Rituals

Designing Rituals of Adoption by Mary Martin Mason (1995: O. J. Howard Publishing) provides excellent guidance for birthparents as well as adoptive parents. Included are specific services, both religious and secular, for moving a child from one family to another.

For example, you might have three candles, a big one symbolizing your child, the other two for the birth and adoptive families. You and the adoptive parents would each light one of the two side candles, then light the child's candle together. The candles, of course, symbolize the uniting of the families. The adoptive parents can then light the big candle each year at the child's birthday celebration.

Vows and promises may be exchanged between birth and adoptive parents, Mason points out. She suggests that gifts be part of the ceremony. Heather described her gifts for her baby:

I made a crib quilt the night before the signing, and I finished at 4 A.M. I also gave him a teddy bear and a book. After it was all over, I went to lunch with my friend.

I said, "You know, I gave him the quilt and the book and the bear, but I didn't give them anything . . ." then I realized I gave them my baby!

A quilt could contain blocks from your family combined with blocks from the adoptive family. Your child would no

doubt cherish his two-family quilt. A birthfamily photo album
or video would also be a lovely gift, as would a journal of
your pregnancy:

> *When I was 71/2 weeks pregnant I started writing a
> journal to my unborn child. I already knew I would
> probably choose adoption, so I wrote why I was making
> that decision. I wrote about who I was and tried to
> answer the questions she might have as to why she was
> adopted.*
>
> *I explained that it wasn't because I didn't love her. It
> was because I did, and I wanted her to have the best. I
> gave my journal to the adoptive parents. They will give
> it to Alex later.*
>
> Katelynn

Mementos from the Hospital

Even as you grieve, you'll probably want mementos of
your baby. You expect the adoptive parents to send you
pictures, but you also may want to take your own while
you're in the hospital. Save the identification card off the
baby's bassinet, keep the wrist bands, press the flowers. You'll
treasure these items later.

Leaving the hospital with empty arms is extremely difficult, birthmothers report. Diane Woodcock, pregnancy counselor, Life for Kids, Winter Park, Florida, talked with women
in her birthparent support group about the pain they experienced as they left the hospital without their baby. "What
might have helped?" she asked.

The women suggested having something to hold such as a
big teddy bear. Not that it would in any way take the place of
the baby, but having something in their arms, "something to
cry into," as several birthmoms expressed it, might help.
Several birthmothers who had lived in one maternity home
during pregnancy mentioned the bear each one was given
when she arrived:

Everybody had a teddy bear to carry around as a friend. I got Cleo, and I still have her. I dress her up with earrings and all that stuff.

Jazmin

Erica and her mother planned a baby shower for Lena, Leif's adoptive mother:

I like to organize things, and I think that helped. I planned a baby shower for Lena at the hospital, and my mom decorated my room. We had balloons and we had gifts.

When they walked in, Lena started crying. She got on the phone and called her friend, and cried, "I'm having a baby shower. I'm having a baby shower." She had thought she'd never have one.

I held Leif all through the shower. They had given me flowers, and their friend had sent flowers. They were happy for Sam and Lena, but they included me, too.

We had a dedication ceremony the next day. There were 19 people there, and we videotaped the whole thing.

I've never been ashamed, and I've never regretted my decision. The fact that my boyfriend and I had a lot of problems during the whole time we dated, and I didn't like his family made it a little easier. We had enough problems ourselves, and I couldn't see putting a baby through that. I couldn't see me 20 years from now with Dan and a baby.

Dan has a brother, and he and his girlfriend had three kids in three years. Their mother is only 16. She had dropped out of school and lived with her mother. Every time I went over there the kids were filthy. I felt for those kids. The mother was so tired. I didn't like what I saw.

Erica

Home from the Hospital

You may be discharged from the hospital before you can legally sign the relinquishment papers. If this happens, you can deal with it in one of several ways.

You can take the baby home with you. You may be able to leave her in the hospital. She can go into a foster home until you sign papers.

Or the adoptive parents can take her home—which is considered a high-risk placement because you could still change your mind about the adoption. Katelynn and her baby's adoptive parents decided they would go ahead with the "high-risk" plan:

> *I didn't like leaving her alone in the hospital, so I had her discharged with me. Then I met Donna and Ted at the same park where we had met earlier. The birthfather and my family were there. I let everybody have a turn holding Alex and saying their last good-byes to her. Everybody was crying their eyes out, and Alex was sound asleep. She had no idea what was going on.*
>
> *I finally built up enough strength to hand her over to Donna and Ted and congratulate them on their baby daughter. As we drove away, I looked back and saw them there in the gazebo holding Alex, and I hoped my little girl would be happy.*
>
> *I heard from them a month later. She had grown a lot and she looked completely different than she had in the hospital.*
>
> Katelynn

Temporary Foster Care

A foster family takes care of children on a short-term basis. The child's birthparents maintain legal custody. Pati used foster care to give her more time to say good-bye to her baby:

> *After delivery it was hard. I never cried so much in*

*my life as when I said good-bye. I put my baby in foster
care for two weeks so I could contemplate and know I
was doing the right thing. I got to change her diaper and
feed her.*

*I went over four or five times during those two weeks.
I was already back at work and didn't have much time.
She is beautiful and I love her to death.*

*During these two weeks Marilou and Don were
scared that I would change my mind. I reassured them
that I needed that time with Leanne. It's one thing to
carry her for nine months. I wanted actually to hold her
after recovering from the sedatives.*

*I didn't want to have any regrets. I didn't want to
think months down the line, "Oh my gosh, I never got to
see my baby." I wanted to feed her. I wanted to dress
her. I did it exactly as I wanted to.*

Carmen and her baby's father agreed that an adoption plan
would be best for their child. However, Carmen simply
couldn't make her final decision before she left the hospital.
Their baby was also placed in foster care:

*I got to spend more time with her because I was in the
hospital for three days because I had a hard time in
delivery. I didn't know if that made it easier or harder.*

*When the adoptive parents came that last day, I sort
of lost it. I started yelling at everyone and said, "I don't
want to do it."*

*She went to a foster home for two days. Then we went
to the agency for the placement. It was harder than I
thought it would be.*

Foster care may be used by a mother who has not decided
whether she wants to keep her baby or place him for adoption.
She may request that the baby be placed in a foster home
while she makes up her mind, as Carmen did.

This can be a good approach if you know you haven't

made a firm decision when the baby is born. Perhaps all you need are two or three days or a couple of weeks to think through your situation. Taylor decided she needed extra time to remake her decision:

I spent three days with Crissy in the hospital. I was her mom during that time, and those were the most important three days of my life. I took care of her constantly and barely slept.

When you're pregnant, you make intellectual decisions, but when you deliver, you start all over. I decided the best thing to do was place Crissie in foster care because I couldn't make a good decision right then.

So she went into foster care and it was so difficult. I felt empty and guilty as I walked out, knowing she needed me. The normal thing would be to leave with a baby in my arms. Instead, I left with a teddy bear.

Christmas was three days later, and it was very different that year. We picked her up at the foster home so an out-of-state brother could meet her. My sister and brothers tried to keep me occupied while my parents took care of her. We visited a friend, and then I decided to bring her home one more time.

By then I think I knew I was going to place her. I sat in my room with the lights low, and explained to her what I was going to do. She was real peaceful in my arms, and I felt she understood, that it was going to be okay.

She went back to her foster home, and I didn't see her for three weeks. During that time I continued counseling and tried to get my life back to normal. Going back to school and dealing with people's comments was hard.

One day I decided I needed to see her again. I went to the foster home, spent two hours with her, took a lot of pictures, talked with her, cried, and, as I left, made my decision.

I was completely numb. I don't remember the 45-minute drive. I didn't share this with anyone except Ric, and I drove to his home and told him.

He said he needed a little more time. That was tough, but I had to respect it. It took him two more weeks, and I didn't even tell my parents during that time.

Last Visit Before Placement

Before I went to see her that last time I had one of my most difficult nights ever. I was crying, going crazy, didn't know what to do. I went downstairs and walked into my parents' room, woke them up, and crawled into bed with my parents. (I was 18.) They cried, and my mom said, "Taylor, we'll help you raise Crissie." That was so wonderful, and then about 30 seconds later reality set in. I didn't want my child raised by grandparents. It wasn't fair to my child. It wasn't fair to my parents.

In the meantime, we looked at families. At that time they were doing semi-open adoption, and we chose a family. A few days before the court date, when she was two months old, two brothers, a sister, and I went back to see her at the foster home for a couple of hours. We took more pictures, and it was time to leave. I was the last one to go.

I said good-bye, and asked God to take care of her. I walked to my car where my brothers and sister were waiting. It was the longest walk of my life.

Although foster care is meant for short-term situations like this, it is often misused. Many children in the United States have been placed in foster care, left there for a long time, years in some cases, while their parents try to "pull themselves together."

In the meantime, the child may be shifted from one foster home to another, never having the love and caring that a permanent family could give him. This is very hard on a child.

The child in foster care keeps his family's name. Foster parents are paid the cost of clothes, room, and board. If the placement is voluntary, the child's parent (or parents) may return at any time, or the child may be transferred to another foster home.

The foster mother, although she may be warm and caring, usually will not allow herself to love the child as if he were her own. This is because he could be—and often is—taken away after a short (or long) period of time.

Children need real parenting, whether from their birth-parents or adoptive parents. Foster care can provide short-term help. For the sake of the child, however, it should never be considered a long-term solution to the possible problems of caring for your child yourself.

Taking the Baby Home

Some birthmothers take their baby home for a few days. In fact, Nancy Johnson, Spokane Consultants in Family Living, reports that about half of their birthmother clients follow this plan. She talked about preparing birthmothers for this difficult period:

"About half of ours take the baby home for a week, some-times two weeks," she said. "One fifteen-year-old birthmom had the baby at home for three weeks. I kept telling the adoptive parents that I thought it would happen, that she'd place. When she was ready, she would know. And she did.

"Some of my older moms say the baby can't enter the front door because they could never let him go. Sometimes the adoptive parents take the baby home at-risk knowing that they may have to return the baby.

"This has such a sense of timing and proactive complete-ness to it. We don't have many moms change their minds because they have laid it out. They say. 'These are the tasks I must complete before I'm done.' She knows she must prepare for separation from the baby. We try to visualize that, who will come, etc.

"If they have had the baby at home for a week or two, we talk about the placement. What will it be like? Some say, 'I have to lay the baby down in her crib, in her own crib.' Others want the adoptive parents to pick her up. Others want to do this in the agency. I have one now where Saturday night the baby will be blessed by the priest. She's one week old, and the birthmom says Saturday night she will turn the baby over to the adoptive parents.

"Sometimes they turn the baby over gradually. One birthmom had the baby home for 2 1/2 weeks. She said, 'I need to see them with him.' So the adoptive couple came over to their home and she put the baby into their arms. When we do it so carefully and proactively, we don't have much mind-changing.

"Rarely do they change their mind in the hospital because they don't have to. I tell her, 'Now you go home, and you will know when it's time.' It's putting trust in them as being competent people. They don't leave their baby in limbo. I tell them their feelings are going to change hourly. At about five or six days they begin to feel like themselves."

Signing the Papers

You may find signing the adoption papers is one of the hardest parts of this whole process. Signing those papers means your adoption plan is now a reality. You may need some additional emotional support at this time.

> *The hardest moment was actually signing the papers. I did it while I held Matthew. My parents had to leave the room because they were crying. Curt was with me and he was crying. I was looking down at Matthew and crying and talking to him, "You're going to have such a wonderful life."*
>
> *I think it was the most selfless thing I have ever done.*

I knew I couldn't give him what they could. It was almost as if it was meant to happen.

We said good-bye and left. I had a lot of closure. I liked seeing him outside the hospital and meeting his parents. I put him in the adoptive mother's arms.

Cerissa

Some birthparents put off signing the consent for adoption. "It seems so final," they may say. If you find you're delaying signing, perhaps you need to discuss with your counselor whether you are considering reclaiming your child, or possibly trying to hold on to control. Know that when you give the adoptive parents their parenting role, as you do when you sign the consent, you are adding to your child's sense of security.

For some birthparents, according to Rachel Waldorf, birthmother and adoption counselor, the signing is not especially traumatic.

"Once you've made the decision, signing the papers is a formality. The baby is already in the birthparents' home. It's a done deal," she pointed out.

Know Your State's Laws

Not all states have the same laws regarding adoption. If you decide to place your baby through an adoption agency, the agency worker will inform you of all the rights you have under the law in your state.

I got to spend two days with her in the hospital, and those were two of the best days of my life. I knew right then, though, that I couldn't be the parent. I didn't have a job. I didn't have a car. I didn't have what you need to be a parent.

My counselor came in just before I left. She read the relinquishment of parental rights, and asked, "Do you know what you are signing?"

I said, "Yes," because she had gone over it with me

before I delivered. It's pretty straightforward, and I
signed it.

Loryna

You generally cannot sign the final adoption papers until after you leave the hospital. However, unless you take your baby home with you, you will be asked to sign a release form in the hospital stating someone else can take the baby away from there. If you release through an agency, this person will be a representative of that agency. This does not mean you have signed away your rights to your child.

The birthparents complete the form for the baby's birth certificate while the mother is still in the hospital. After the adoption is finalized, a new birth certificate is issued. In this one, the adoptive parents are listed as if the baby had been born to them.

The first birth certificate, the one with the birthparents' names on it, is "sealed"—filed away where it cannot be seen except by order of the court. However, the sealed record laws are changing, and may not be in effect in your state.

In agency adoption, relinquishment becomes "final and binding" (you can't change your mind about releasing your child) when these signed papers are filed by the agency with the State Department of Social Services. Once both of you have signed the adoption papers and the adoption plan has been accepted by the State Department of Social Services, generally you no longer have any legal rights or responsibility for your child.

Meeting the adoptive parents does not, of course, change the finality of actual relinquishment. In open adoption, however, you and the adoptive parents may agree that continued contact with the child is an important responsibility you still have. As you say good-bye, perhaps you and the adoptive parents will plan a time soon when you can see your child again.

CHAPTER 12

Grieving the Loss of Your Baby

Driving home from the hospital with Nick and my parents, I said I just don't want to live the next two years. There were nights after that that I'd wake up screaming. There was no relief from the pain. I'd scream because I couldn't express in any other way how it felt not to have her there.

My arms would physically ache, and my chest would feel like it would explode. I had to take it by ten-minute segments. I can survive for ten minutes. Then life sort of went on.

If I had chosen to parent Jenae, I would be dealing with different losses—everybody has losses. I don't regret my decision. I miss her incredibly much and grieve the part of her life that I will never be able to experience. I will never have the experience of her as

*a child, as a baby. All I have are the three days with
her in the hospital, which I cherish.*

Kathleen

*I wish I had had somebody to talk with that would tell
me about grief. My heart hurt, and why would my heart
hurt if I was doing the right thing?*

*When I started being on a panel and talking in the
high schools about my experience, I felt better.*

*I think anybody who is going to place a child should
have some counseling before they place.*

Alvera

*The day of placement was real rough. I cried most of
the day. I was still enjoying being with Dakota, but I was
realizing our time together was almost over. We signed
the papers in the hospital, and then we all went over to
the agency where we had another two hours with
the baby.*

*We walked down the hall to the room where the
adoptive parents were waiting. Steve carried Dakota,
and he placed her in their arms. We took some pictures,
and then we left. That's when they had the placement
ceremony. We had made a tape of us reading a poem
about giving them this wonderful gift.*

*Before Dakota was born we had made the tape. We
wrote a letter to the baby, and we did a lot of talking
with the adoption counselor. She tried to give us an idea
of what it would be like. I have always been a pretty
emotional person, and I'm able to express my sadness. I
cry, and I think that's helpful.*

*After we left the agency, I thought I'd just go home,
get in bed, and cry the day away. But we stopped at the
counselor's office first and talked to her for a few
minutes. I was sad but talking with her helped.*

On the way home we dropped the film off to be

*developed. Then we rented a movie and ordered pizza. I
thought it would be a wasted day, but there were some
positive feelings there.*

*It went pretty well from then on. I had a lot of prepa-
ration in dealing with my grief before Dakota was born.
I cried a lot, but it got easier after awhile.*

Sabrina

You *Will* Grieve

Is it ever easy to release a baby for adoption? *Of course
not!*

Releasing a baby for adoption causes emotions similar to
those a mother feels if she loses her baby through death. The
birthparent will go through the same kind of grieving process.
If she doesn't, if she simply pushes her grief out of her mind
and "forgets the whole thing," she may have emotional
problems later.

Carmen thought she was dealing with her depression. She
went back to school and figured that would help. But she
couldn't handle the comments:

*I don't remember crying at the placement ceremony.
In fact, I don't remember anything that day. I was in a
daze. I gave Star to them, and I felt detached from the
whole thing.*

*I went to a friend's house for the weekend and didn't
think much about it. Two days later my mom took me
shopping, and I lost it, right there in the middle of
the mall.*

*I went back to school four weeks after Star was born.
It was probably better that I got out, got my mind on
other things, didn't have time to sit around and be totally
depressed.*

*It's been hard for me to deal with kids, my friends at
school making comments. My close friends were supportive, but a lot of people weren't. I can't tell you how*

*many times I've heard, "How could you do that?" I got
sick of people talking down to me.*

*By the end of September, I went into this deep depres-
sion. Before that I was in denial. It wasn't that I forgot
about Star, but I went out and did other things. Then it
hit me all of a sudden. I quit going to school, and
haven't gotten back yet. She's six months old now.*

*I'm going to try to get in a special half-day school
program where you stay in one classroom the whole
time. I'm supposed to be in tenth grade but I'm a year
behind. I don't want to go back into regular classes.*

*I'm going to be sad about the adoption, no matter
what, but no matter what anybody says, I can still know
in my heart I did what was right for me.*

Carmen is now participating in birthparent panels, and this
allows her a safe space to talk about her experience. She says
she wants to get the message out about the love that goes into
an adoption decision. Doing so helps her cope with her grief.

No matter how sure you are that your adoption plan is right
for your baby and right for you, no matter how much you trust
the adoptive parents you select, you *will* grieve the loss of
your baby. Even if the adoption is completely open and you
visit your child periodically, you are still losing your role as a
parent. You have traded that role for the role of birthparent.
No matter how good a decision this is, you will grieve.

*It was a Friday night when my mom drove me home
from the hospital. We stopped at the store and I waited
in the car because I had been crying. I watched kids pull
up in the parking lot, laughing and talking, and I
thought, how can they be having a good time?*

*We went on home, and my mom tucked me into bed
and stroked my head while I fell asleep. I needed that.*

*I got involved with other birthmothers through the
agency. A couple of months after Jessica was born I*

spoke to a group of prospective adoptive parents.
Talking about it helped. I let my friends know that if they
had questions, they should ask. I didn't want anyone's
pity, but I wanted them there for me.

Maggie

Maggie, like most birthparents, found that photos and
letters from the adoptive parents were extremely important
to her:

After I went home, I checked that mail every single
day, hoping for those first pictures. And they came in
about a week. That first year Mark and Kathi wrote
every couple of months, and that helped. The past two
years it has slowed down, but I don't need it now like I
did in the beginning. They sent me a video of Jessica
when she was two. Their letters are very descriptive.

As time went by, I was all right with it.

Grief May Be Immediate

Sonia reacted dramatically to her depression immediately
after placing her baby:

I told Joshua good-bye and gave him to the adoptive
parents. I went home.

When I got there, I lay on my bed with my picture of
Joshua, and I cried for three hours. Then I trashed my
room. I was crying and I was saying, "I'm sorry, I'm
sorry." I even kicked a hole in my wall.

After that, I was much better. Later when I was in
counseling, she said this anger often happens, but
usually it's later.

When I woke up the next morning, my mom tried to
help. She was taking it real hard, too, because this was
her first grandson. I realized I had to take it one step at
a time. I learned that if you really love something, you
sometimes have to let it go. I knew that as the days went

by it would get better. And it did, although I still have my moments, like on Joshua's birthday, Mother's Day, and Christmas. Christmas is real real hard.

I'll never forget crying in my room that night. I know that helped me. I was really letting him go that night.

I went back to my high school two weeks after he was born and talked to one of my classes. It was hard. I had disappeared, and I came back and told them my story. People were a lot more sensitive, more understanding after that.

Going on panels helps me. I still do that.

Seeing how happy Travis and Vanessa were gave me strength to get through those first few months, those hard hard months. You go through a period of mourning. I lost him, but knowing they were so happy helped me.

I saw him a year later when they came to my house. I told myself I would be calm, cool and collected, but as soon as they got here, I ran out and grabbed Joshua out of his car seat and hugged him. I see them once or twice a year and hear from them every couple of months.

If you don't go through counseling during this period, I think it's really going to hurt you. I started going to Parenting Resources a week after placement. I went there five or six months, and that helped a lot.

Delayed Reaction to Placement

Alexis' hardest time was a month or so after placement:

At first I was okay. Betsy was gone and my problem was solved. I was tired of crying. I didn't want to cry any more.

Then it hit me again, one night about a month later. I tried to call a friend but she wasn't home. The only people I could reach were Troy and Cynthia, the adoptive parents. I was so upset, and we talked for awhile.

They called back the next day and said, "Do you

want to come see her?" So I went up to see them, and that helped. I had thought it would be better not to see Betsy, but now I wish I had gone a couple of weeks after they took her home.

Leaving her after that visit was just like leaving the hospital. It was this huge ache like I had when I broke up with my first love. But I knew that pain, and I knew I could deal with it.

My stepmom said each night for awhile when she would come home, she'd find me depressed. The adoption service doesn't focus much on post-placement counseling, and I think they should.

For the adoptive parents to suggest that Alexis visit the baby while she was so depressed took courage and a lot of love for their child and their child's birthmother. The adoption was not finalized at this time. Troy, the adoptive father, explained later:

We really believe in the open adoption concept. We also knew that if Alexis got the feeling we were trying to cut her off, it could stop the adoption.

We started out wanting openness for the sake of our child. Now it's a pleasant relationship which is also to our benefit.

Lisette placed her baby seven years ago, and she was not encouraged to choose the family herself. In fact, she had no opportunity to do so. Leaving the baby was extremely hard:

I was at the lowest point after I left the hospital. James wasn't with me, and I felt like I had forgotten something. For several days I was a basket case.

Finally one day I got this feeling of peace. The phone rang a couple of hours later, and the adoption counselor said they had placed him. She told me about the family, and I was happy for them. They wrote me a beautiful letter, thanking me, and saying they wanted to keep contact.

When I went back to school I kept getting, "Where's your baby? I don't see him in day care."

I'd say, "I placed him for adoption."

They would say, "Oh, I'm so sorry," as if somebody had died.

I wrote an article for the school paper, and they ran it with a picture of the baby. I described what happened and said it's a positive situation, I'm not a freak. Nobody died. As a matter of fact, somebody lived because of this. I wanted people to realize adoption is not a bad thing.

I always tell kids it's not something I would wish on anyone because the pain is there. But you need to understand life is what you make it. You can't spend your life wallowing in "I have a child and I don't have him . . ." You have to think of what's best for yourself as well as what's best for your child.

The days immediately following placement were hardest for Cerissa:

I had a real hard time a few days afterward with post-partum depression. If I saw a pregnant woman, I was totally out of it.

It wasn't that I wanted to keep him. Even though my mother offered to help, I knew it wouldn't be good for him. But the feeling of life inside me was so incredible that it was hard seeing other women pregnant, and I didn't have that any longer.

Maria and Ken wrote letters and sent pictures constantly. We have four videotapes. I feel I know his entire family. Everyone looks at the camera and says, "Hi, Cerissa."

When Matthew was 4, he looked at the camera and said, "Hi, Cerissa. I love you." He took my prom picture to school and said, "This is my birthmom."

Hurting Doesn't Mean It's the Wrong Decision

If we do something that hurts a lot, we tend to think the act must be wrong. A birthmother may think, "I'm feeling terrible. If it hurts to release my baby for adoption, why should I do it? It must be a poor decision."

Carrying out an adoption plan is an extremely difficult thing to do. If you decide to release your baby for adoption, of course you'll hurt. You need to realize, and your family needs to realize, that this is absolutely normal. It does not mean you've made a poor decision. You're losing a baby. But the hurt will gradually go away—as long as you face your grief and don't try to bury it.

> *A part of you shuts down to survive. It was incredibly hard. Part of moving out of state was to start a new life, but that doesn't work. It's especially hard this time of year because Jenae's birthday is this month.*
>
> Kathleen

The best therapy while in this situation—you're hurting and you wonder if it will ever stop—is to talk with another birthmother. Perhaps someone who released her baby several years ago will share with you how she feels now about her decision. Not that you will ever feel exactly like someone else, but it often helps to share experiences.

You may also find it helps to write your child a letter telling her how much you love her. You can let her know that it's precisely for that reason you're letting someone else love and care for her.

Often the baby's father needs to grieve too. Of course these suggestions also apply to birthfathers. Talking with another birthfather might have helped Erik:

> *After placement it was an emotional roller coaster. I was glad it was behind us. I didn't realize how emotional it would be.*
>
> *The first two weeks were really tough, but it gradually*

*tapered off after that. But it came up occasionally with a
comment, "You made me give my baby away."*

*Neither of us ever had any counseling after she was
born.*

It's important that the birthparents, especially if they're still
together, make the adoption plan together. Otherwise, there
may be some blaming afterward—"You made me give my
baby away." Erik and his baby's mother were together for
awhile after placement, but eventually split up.

Fathers are likely to experience *denial* of grief more
intensely and for a longer period of time than do the mothers.
This may give others (and themselves) the impression that
they aren't experiencing any effects from the loss of the baby.

The father may simply be behind time in his grieving. He
may not experience the reality of the child until birth occurs.
To the mother, the child was real throughout pregnancy, and
her feelings of parenthood become even more intense at birth.
If her child is released for adoption, she will grieve. The
father may not . . . until later.

Help with Grieving

There are several books that might help you get through
this time. *How to Survive the Loss of a Love* by Melba
Colgrove, et al. (1993: Prelude Press), *Given in Love* by
Maureen Connelly (1990: Centering Corporation), and *Saying
Goodbye to a Baby: A Book About Loss and Grief in Adoption*
by Patricia Roles (1989: Child Welfare League of America)
are examples.

As mentioned before, talking with other birthparents is
especially valuable:

*I really haven't had a hard time, probably because
I've had a lot of support. Keeping in touch with the
agency helped me a lot. If I'm having a hard time, I go
to a birthparent support group meeting.*

I have my down times, everybody does, but you have to think about the benefits. My child is getting on with her life and I'm getting on with mine. I can't dwell on the fact that I don't have my child.

I think about Melissa every day, but every time I look at her pictures, every time I show those pictures to people, it helps me cope with it. Talking about it helps, too, and that's why I'm doing these panels. The more I talk about it, the better I am.

People say I should just forget her, get on with my life. I can't do that. I can't keep it a secret. It's part of who I am, part of my past.

That's how the old adoptions were—nobody talked about it. It was terrible, and it's those people who are having problems, people who tried to put it behind them. They are the ones who cry every time they talk about their baby.

Loryna

Several birthparents quoted here have been extremely positive about birthparent support groups. These groups generally are there to offer comfort and sympathy for your feelings, and give you an opportunity to talk with others and exchange information about adoption.

If you aren't aware of such a group, check with your adoption counselor. If that doesn't work, call a local adoption agency or adoption facilitator. CUB (Concerned United Birthparents) is an organization of birthparents. CUB support groups are active in many communities. For information, check your phone directory or call 515/263-9558.

For some, the support group is one of the few places where everyone understands the birthparent's point of view, and where people express their feelings openly. If you're feeling alone in your adoption grief, you might find a birthparent support group extremely helpful.

CHAPTER 13

What's Ahead?
Planning Your Future

*We get lots of pictures—I'm starting my second
scrapbook now. We've been together three times since
Dakota was born, and they're coming to my graduation
in May. Those letters and pictures are so helpful.*

*Two weeks after Dakota's birth we got pictures of the
placement ceremony with a letter about how she was
doing at home. That helped a lot. They still write every
month. We write back, and I send pictures of us and tell
them how we're doing. I want to stay in contact always.*

*My grandma is real supportive. She sends letters and
pictures to Dakota, and I share the ones I get with
Grandma. She's coming for my graduation, and she'll
meet Dakota and her adoptive parents. She loves Dakota
so much even though she hasn't met her.*

Sabrina

*The first month was difficult, but it was never unbear-
able. When I started feeling low, I would look at my
pictures and I would know Leif was fine. When I was
really low, we would visit Dan's brother and his girlfriend and their three kids with all their problems.*

I have never regretted the adoption.

*I see a five-year-old now, and I wonder, "Oh my God,
what would I do with a five-year-old? They're terrors."
Not that they're bad kids, but it's hard for their parents.*

*One reason it's worked so well is that we suggested
how we wanted the adoption to happen, and Sam and
Lena picked up on it. For awhile they called every ten
days. How much they love Leif helped.*

*Leif knows now that he came out of my tummy. My
aunt sends them a special ornament every year at
Christmas. Lena says when she talks on adoption
panels, she says, "Don't fear the birthparents. When you
work with them, you're repaid a thousand times."*

                                                                  Erica

*I have pictures of Scotty in my room. It's not like I'm
trying to shut him out. There's a part of me that's gone,
but I know he's happy, he's healthy, and he's loved. I'm
not going to sit around and cry about it. If you do, you
don't get on with your life. I need to get on with my
plans and my life.*

                                                                Kernisha

Will You Visit Each Other?

Many of the birthparents quoted here feel it is important to
continue contact with their child and his adoptive family. For
some, it's pictures several times a year and perhaps getting
together annually. For others, it's more frequent contact,
especially at first. Emily commented:

*Louita is 18 months old now, and I talk with her
parents every week or two. I saw her a lot the first year*

— at three weeks, six weeks, Christmas, her baptism, my graduation from college, her first birthday, my birthday. I have only seen her twice since her birthday but I don't have the need now that I did.

This is so much different from my first child's adoption. Evan's parents stopped writing me after the first couple of letters. It's easier to focus on Louita because I see her, but I certainly don't forget about Evan. I pray for both my kids every night. Having Louita's adoption so open makes it a little easier to deal with Evan's because I see how well she's doing.

Emily and Maggie discussed the benefits of staying involved in the adoption community:

I find a lot of connection in the adoption community. The adoption support group through the Crisis Pregnancy Center here helped me. Getting your questions answered is important.

Being on the school panels helps me because I'm out there talking about it. I'm not bottling it up inside, and I feel good about it. Working in the mentoring program is good, too, because I can reaffirm my decision.

Emily

It's important to educate people about adoption so they don't have these stereotypes of birthparents, that they don't love their children. I spoke about adoption at a high school a year or so ago, and these 15-16-year-olds asked a lot of questions.

One boy was especially curious. He asked, "Do you think about her? Do you miss her?"

I said, "I think about her every day," and he got tears in his eyes. The teacher told me later that he was adopted.

Maggie

Keeping Communication Open

Many birthparents feel that without open adoption, they would not be able to let their child go to another family. Probably the biggest reason for continuing contact between the birthparents and the adoptive parents, however, is the benefit to the child. One's birth heritage is important, and during the closed adoption era, adoptees often felt they lost that heritage.

For some families, frequent letters and pictures help the adoptee stay in touch with his birth heritage. This was the case with Yvette—at first:

> *The adoptive parents and I talked for awhile and I met their two-year-old son. They took pictures of me with them so they could show Rosie as she grows up.*
>
> *They send letters and pictures, and say it was a match made in heaven. She sent pictures of the two kids fighting like me and my brother used to do.*
>
> *We wrote back and forth every other week those first six months, and I liked that. Then we moved on to less often. My mother said it's about time to let go, to let up on the contact, so I waited for three months. I feel the contact will continue although I haven't heard from them now for two years.*
>
> *I want them to know I haven't forgotten about them. I think they were waiting on me. They were sending me pictures as long as I wrote to them.*
>
> Yvette

It's important that you be able to go on with your life without your child. You'll always think of her, probably every day, but your focus may change. You may find you need less contact as the months and years go by.

I wonder about Yvette's mother's advice, however, "It's about time to let go, let up on the contact." If you expect weekly, or even monthly contact forever, you and/or the adoptive parents are likely to have trouble fulfilling your promise. Your child will be ahead, however, if you and the adoptive parents do stay in contact. You don't want your child to think you've forgotten her.

It's easy for communication to stop because one side doesn't get around to writing. The other person doesn't write "until I hear from them." And that's all it takes to lose communication with each other, as Yvette and her child's adoptive parents appear to be doing. You'll all probably be happier if you don't let that happen.

> *We communicate regularly with the adoptive parents. We scrapped the agency right away because we just didn't need it to pass letters back and forth between us.*
>
> *I know the adoptive mother was really worried we might want him back. But we love those guys. They are family. I know this is the right thing, and we have a very special relationship with them.*
>
> David

If You Don't Have Contact at First

If you choose not to meet with the adoptive parents after placement, you might find you would like to do so at a later date. It's best always to keep communication as open as possible so that you'll be able to make changes in your contact agreement.

Nick's birthdaughter is 7, and he has received yearly updates. He's written only one letter and sent pictures and some gifts. He explained why he may get more involved:

> *I always assumed they just wanted to send updates and not hear much from us. Now there's a new social worker on the case who's more concerned with what's best for our daughter and what's best for us. He feels it might be best to communicate back and forth more.*
>
> *I plan to send a letter soon updating my life. I just graduated from college, I'm working, married, and have*

*a child on the way. The social worker suggested I share
these things and explain what I'm like because often the
child is concerned about where they came from, where
they get personality or behavior quirks.*

Eddie's adoption was closed for ten years. Four years ago
he told his adoptive mother he would like to meet his
birthmom. After a brief search, they met, and the relationship
is going well. Eddie, now 14, commented:

*First of all, I feel happy. I don't consider her my
mother. I think of Maya as a real special friend. It's more
than a regular friend because I know how we're related.*

*Before I met her, all I knew was her name was Maya.
I always wondered, where do I get my personality? Why
do I look the way I look?*

*I've met a lot of people from Maya's family and they
feel like family, too. I call Maya and she calls me back.
We go out for lunch or dinner, and we go shopping.*

*I don't think too much about being adopted. I think
it's pretty normal. I'm glad Maya placed me for adoption. If she hadn't—I know she doesn't have much money
now, and it would have been real hard for both of us. I
like being in my adoptive family.*

Maya also talked about their relationship:

*Eddie and I are great friends. People try to describe
our relationship like an aunt or a friend, but I think you
really have to say it's a birthmom relationship. I'm
really not an aunt. I'm Eddie's birthmom, and that's a
special relationship.*

What Should He Call You?

Will your child know you as his birthparents? One of the
advantages of open adoption is the honesty involved. You and
the adoptive parents will probably decide it's best to be honest

in your relationship with your child. That includes openness
about who you are. Rita discussed this issue:

> *In open adoption, I think it's best to tell them, "You
> have four parents—a mommy and daddy you live with,
> and you also have Rita and David, your other mommy
> and daddy who let us raise you. Most kids get only two
> parents. You're so loved you have four."*
>
> *The thing that means the most to me is getting pic-
> tures of him. There can never be enough pictures. The
> letters are nice, and I enjoy talking with them on the
> phone, but the pictures are something I can look at all
> the time and know how happy he is.*

"Pictures" in some open adoptions may simply mean
pictures of the child the adoptive parents send to the
birthparents. It's a good idea, however, for birthparents to
send pictures to the child regularly, too. He's much less likely
to feel alienated from his biological heritage if he has photos
of his birthfamily as the years go by.

> *I'm working on slides my dad took when I was
> growing up, and I'm going to make a video for my baby,
> "This Is My Life." I went to Disney World last month. I
> got him some mouse ears and sent them with a note. I
> don't want him to forget me.*

> Heather

Coping with Family Attitudes

You may have to face negative remarks from friends and
family after your child goes to the adoptive family. A year
after placement, a chance remark from a relative caused David
and Rita's grieving to resurface with a vengeance. David said:

> *We probably dealt with the grief a year later. We knew
> it was the right decision, and we had a lot of love and
> support around us. That helped. But there was one
> person, an aunt, who commented, "How could you give*

up that child?" At that point, I think all the doubts that
had not been there came flooding in to both of us. That's
when we knew we had to get some counseling to deal
with it.

My counseling came from my pastor. We knew this
was the right decision, and this was where the rubber
meets the road. What you start, you finish, and we just
hung on. It got better day by day.

Annette, whose child was almost four years old when she
placed him, had a particularly difficult time coping with her
family's attitudes:

I lost a lot of my family when I placed him. Finally,
a couple of months after he was gone, I told them,
"You need to listen to me." I told them to look at my
situation. Life was getting harder and harder and my
little boy was suffering.

They said, "All you have to do is work and take
care of him."

I said, "Look, everybody is yelling at me, but I
don't hear anybody offering to help." I told them it
wasn't because I didn't care. I did it because I love
him and I want him to have a future. Some of my
family understands now.

I have a lot of friends who are young and trying to
raise kids. Some finally said to me, "You know, you're
right."

The biggest fear in placing seems to be "What will
my family think?" But the important thing is what do
you think of yourself? You're the one who has to live
with it.

Talking about your child will probably help you deal with
his absence. If you have supportive family and friends, you
have a great resource. If you don't, it may be especially
important for you to join a birthparent support group.

Writing Your Feelings

Do you write your feelings, perhaps in journal fashion, stories or poetry? Or perhaps you'll write letters to your child. Even if you have your child's address, you may choose not to send some of your letters to her at this time. Simply writing out one's feelings sometimes makes one feel better. Your birthchild might like to see your letters at some future time.

> *We met the summer James was 5. He chose a picture of the two of us for a calendar for his mom. He said, "That's the woman whose belly I grew in."*
>
> *We're going to meet in Colorado next year. We all love each other, but we're afraid we'll infringe on each others' lives. They say, "If it's okay with you . . ." and I say, "If it's okay with you . . ."*
>
> *A couple of years ago I sent James a baseball jersey and he wrote me a thank-you letter himself. The first line was "I'm very glad you had me for your baby. Thank you very much and I love you." He signed it with a big purple marker. He's in the first grade now.*
>
> Lisette

You're likely to find certain days especially hard. Birthparents often mention the holiday season as being a time they mourn their child's loss. So is Mother's Day or Father's Day. Your child's birthday is another time you're especially likely to miss him. Perhaps you'll develop a ceremony, either private or with friends or family members, to celebrate your child at these times. Family support can mean a great deal to grieving birthparents as Tatum pointed out:

> *My mother works real hard to keep me occupied on those three difficult days—Mother's Day, baby's birthday, and Christmas. One year she sent me flowers on my baby's birthday. Nobody else knew what they meant. That was important, to have somebody say, "You did the right thing."*

What About You?

If you give your child another family, you will continue to think about him. You'll continue to love him.

But what about you? Your life will probably always "feel" different because of your birthchild. Does this mean you have different goals than you did before you got pregnant? Or will your life continue much as it was?

If you haven't graduated from high school, are you working toward that goal? Did you stay in school throughout your pregnancy? If not, have you returned? Or are you working toward a GED (General Education Diploma)? If not, your next step may be in that direction.

Sometimes a very young birthmother may find herself wanting the adoptive parents to parent *her* as well as her child. This generally would not be a reasonable expectation. After the placement, you want the adoptive parents to focus on parenting your child. You will continue to love your child, and to be in some way a part of their lives. You will, however, go on with your own life while their energies go to the child.

Perhaps you've finished high school. Is college part of your plan? What about your career? If you feel you need job training, but don't know what you want to do, check with your high school or college career center.

If you have other children, perhaps you would be interested in some parenting classes. You already know how rapidly children change, and how important it is that parents be ready for those changes. Actually, you may want to attend some parenting classes or at least read about children's development even if you're not rearing a child yourself. If you spend time with your child and her adoptive family, knowing something about her development will make it easier to interact with her.

One birthmother was hurt when she visited her nine-month-old birthdaughter. The little girl was in the middle of the "stranger anxiety" stage so typical at this age. At this point, her birthmother was one of those strangers. "She didn't even want much to do with her (adoptive) father," her adoptive mother said ruefully.

If this birthmom had realized her daughter would be hitting this don't-touch-me stage about this time, she might have been able to accept her daughter's standoffishness more easily. Knowing something about babies' and toddlers' development will help you build rapport with your birthchild because you'll have an idea of the kinds of things she's likely to enjoy at her current stage.

Whether you are placing your baby soon after delivery, or he's already several months or several years old, you'll feel a void in your life when he's gone.

> *It took me time to deal with losing Rosie. At first I felt empty. There was this void in my life, and the letters and pictures helped fill that space.*
>
> *Now there is still that little empty space, but it's not sad or dark, it's just that a part of me is someplace else. I think about Rosie all the time. I sit and look at her picture and wonder if she's like me.*
>
> Yvette

Working toward your goals and your dreams will help fill that void. Knowing you gave your child a loving adoptive family is reassuring, especially if you continue communicating with them. Your child will grow up knowing his birthparents made a loving decision for his welfare, and that their love continues.

One of the advantages of giving your child an adoptive family is the chance it gives you to focus on yourself, your growth, your own development. You don't want to let feelings of loss or depression keep you from going ahead with your own life. Get whatever help you can, whether it's more education, career development, or in other areas of your life. You've made a plan for your baby and she is being taken care of in the best way possible. Now it's time to focus on *you*.

CHAPTER 14

Open Adoption Joins Families

Many people endured lots of pain in the days of closed adoption. Of course open adoption is not a guarantee that the pain will be missing. Sometimes open adoption doesn't work very well, and sometimes the openness simply doesn't continue. Birthmothers have shared their grief here of open doors slammed shut by adoptive parents. Adoptive parents speak of their sorrow when they have no contact from their child's birthparents. There is no guarantee.

Birthparents have made many suggestions in these pages on carefully choosing your child's adoptive parents and building and maintaining a good relationship with them. Many of the 39 birthparents I interviewed feel extremely positive about the success of their adoption plan. Adoptive parents have also shared their strong feelings about the importance of continuing contact with their child's birthparents.

Gary and Joyce were one of these couples. I called April
first, and asked if I might interview her. She hesitated, then
said she would like to speak to her child's adoptive parents
first. I was to call her back a few days later. I was a little put
off—if she didn't want to talk with me, fine, but I was concerned that she felt she had no right to do so unless the adoptive parents approved. I didn't like that—once more the
birthparent was in the shadow.

How wrong I was! An open adoption relationship depends
tremendously on each person's sensitivity to the needs and
desires of the others. April knew very well she had every *right*
to talk with me. If doing so made her child's adoptive parents
the least bit uncomfortable, however, that was reason enough
to refuse my request.

A few days later she said she would be happy to talk with
me, and that I could call her child's parents, Gary and Joyce,
if I wished. I did, and offered to send them a book I had
written about open adoption. I sensed they would like to be
reassured that I wasn't out to sensationalize their story.

After they saw my other book, they said they would talk
with me, too.

The love, caring concern, and sensitivity to each other's
feelings in these families is what open adoption is all about. I
am delighted to share their story here:

April—Pregnant at Graduation

*When I was 21, three days before I graduated from
college three years ago, I found out I was pregnant. I
was shocked, didn't want to admit it. The relationship
with the father was not a good one. We were friends but
nothing beyond that.*

*I could not believe I was pregnant. I came from a
strong Christian background where one of the worst
things you could do is get pregnant while you're single. I
told my sister the night before I graduated. She was very*

surprised, and very supportive. She was the first one to demonstrate that family love is unconditional.

I considered all my options. I briefly considered abortion even though up until that time I was very much pro-life. Several of my friends who had had abortions encouraged me to terminate. I decided to continue the pregnancy, but I knew it was my obligation to look at all the options.

When he found out I was pregnant, the baby's father didn't want to believe it. He said he'd support me in whatever I wanted to do but he obviously did not want to be involved. I spoke to him once or twice during the pregnancy, but that was it. He signed the adoption papers without knowing much about it. He knew what I was doing. He made his choices and I made mine.

I was very cautious at first when I looked at adoption. I had heard many nightmare stories. My best friend in high school was adopted, and she was real bitter toward her birthmother, and very angry. A piece of her was missing. So I was skeptical because I didn't want my child to feel like Audrey felt.

Researching Adoption

First I called a group involved in adoption and learned about different types of adoption, closed versus open. Then I called a couple of attorneys, and realized I wanted an agency. One of my main concerns was how the parents would handle the child's feelings toward adoption. How will they deal with a teenager angry about adoption? It was important to me that the couple be researched and prepared for parenthood.

Another concern was that some agencies would let me see portfolios of the couples but not meet them. Anybody can look good in a picture and sound good in a letter, but I needed to meet them. I trust my intuition a lot. It was important to interview them and learn that they are real people. Most of all I wanted them to know something about me, that I was a real person.

I consulted at least 15 agencies and adoption services. It was funny how little things could turn me off. I decided on this agency because they seemed genuine. They gave the parents a lot of preparation, and they weren't just saying what I wanted to hear. So from there, I turned a lot of it over to them although I always felt I was in complete control.

When I did all this calling I hadn't yet decided on adoption. I knew I could give this child money, and I could give this child love, but the big thing I couldn't give him was a father. I have worked so much with children, and I have seen what a bad home life can do. For him I wanted the best. I soon knew adoption was what I needed to do.

You have to get your facts together. For anything in life you do your research. I didn't know much about adoption, just the black cloud of what happened to Audrey.

Choosing My Baby's Parents

I read a lot of portfolios and I interviewed several couples. My doctor suggested somebody, and so did my sister. I got a number of letters, but I stuck close to the agency.

The first two couples I interviewed were wonderful people, but they were not the couple for me.

Then my social worker said, "There is one more couple, and they're now finishing their letter." I read their letter, and it seemed different from the others. It was this incredible love shining forth. Joyce said she had never doubted Gary's love for her, and what a bold statement that was. We had a lot in common—Gary's

*love for music, he's a principal and I'm a teacher, our
love for animals, all kinds of things.*

*They were wonderful. They were also funny, and I
felt comfortable with making them laugh. They were
incredible.*

*I didn't tell them right away because I knew that as
soon as I told them, I would have given my word. I
would stick with that even though it wasn't yet a legal
obligation. Three days later I called the agency and they
told Joyce and Gary. I was seven months pregnant by
then.*

*The agency set up a second meeting Thanksgiving
weekend. I was very nervous. I didn't know what would
come out of this meeting. My counselor asked how much
openness I wanted, and I didn't know. She asked if I
wanted visitation and I said no.*

*At the end of that meeting Gary said, "We haven't
talked about how much openness, but we want you to
know that any time you want to call or visit, you are
welcome." I was skeptical. Why would they want that?*

Meeting the Extended Family

*We set up another meeting so they could meet my
parents and my sister. I'm very close to my parents, and
I wanted them to meet Gary and Joyce.*

*Then it was my turn to meet their parents. I was
nervous—a basket case. They invited me over to their
home which amazed me. When I met Joyce's mother, I
stuck my hand out to shake hers. Instead, she embraced
me and said, "We can't begin to tell you how wonderful
a gift this is for Joyce and Gary."*

*The day after Joyce met me she bought a blanket with
bunnies on it for the baby. Then at Christmas the year
after Jon was born, she gave me a sweater with the
same design.*

Preparing for Birth

I wanted Joyce and Gary to be there during the labor and delivery. As soon as Jon was born, I wanted him to hear his parents' voices.

We went through the labor classes together, and through that we got closer. The friendship that developed was amazing, a real closeness. Joyce started coming to the doctor's office with me, and Gary came to one of the ultrasound appointments. It worked out real real well.

I was two weeks late, and the doctor found out I was actually in labor. Joyce and Gary were with me from the very beginning—the coldest day of the year. My father was out of town at that time, but they got to know my mother better.

I will always remember their faces after Jon was born. Gary just couldn't keep his eyes off his son. It was amazing.

After I was taken to my room, Gary and Joyce came in and asked if I was sure of my decision. If I wasn't, they were fine with it. They didn't want me to feel any pressure. My answer was that I had never been more positive.

We all got a chance to hold Jon, and then they went home and rested. Joyce's parents came up, and my father came back and saw Jon.

I was in the hospital for 48 hours. The first night everybody went home and I kept Jon in my room all night. I spent a lot of time one on one with him, and that was important to me. He was an amazing baby, a real neat baby. The second night my sister stayed with me. I can't tell you the peace I felt in my heart.

The last day in the hospital there were a lot of tears, tears of emotion, but not of sadness. One nurse asked if I was sure, that I seemed unhappy, and I said I was sure.

Visits After Placement

Jon needed to stay in the hospital two days longer, and Joyce and Gary stayed with him. Gary delivered the baby pictures to me the day they took him home. He said I had an eternal invitation to their home. I guess that's when I really believed them. We made plans to celebrate his one-week birthday together, and we had a great time. My sister went with me, and it was wonderful seeing him there. We also went over for his one-month birthday.

Jon has a baby quilt made of different memory scraps, and they asked for a piece of our family tartan to put in the quilt.

That first week after he was born, I was at peace. I knew I had done the right thing, I knew he was happy. I knew I had done what God wanted me to do. I never once regretted my decision. It was one of those few times in your life that you know you made the right decision.

I went through the grieving process while I was still pregnant. I went through that when I was interviewing, and I went through it when I chose Gary and Joyce. But afterward, no. I think the thing I hear from people is that they miss the child a lot, but I wasn't ready to parent. I will be a good mother some day, but when he was born, I wasn't ready.

My biggest worry was that Jon wouldn't know I love him, but he knew that from the beginning.

A "Natural" Friendship

I think people are scared of what they don't know, and I had answers to my questions. He was two in January, and I see him a lot. It's a natural friendship. When our lives are busy, we don't see each other a lot; when we have more time, we're together more. I don't think there has been a two-month period when we haven't seen each other. Joyce says you can never have too many people loving a child. Jon refers to my parents as Grandma and Grandpa, and my sister is aunt. I'm April.

For his one-year birthday we went on a trip to Des Moines, and they gave me a necklace with a triangle in it representing the adoption. They sent me a bouquet of flowers on his first birthday. They are part of my family.

This year for his second birthday we celebrated together with his cousins and other relatives. We've learned that if parents and other adults are comfortable with the situation, the children are, too. When parents are fearful and worried and anxious, children do the same.

My life has been wonderful since then. This is my second year of teaching. I started teaching the day the adoption was finalized.

I think the adoptive parent education groups are so important. The parents talk to birthparents and to adoptive parents. It's interesting seeing people at different stages of the process. You see a lot of fear with some people, excitement with others. It was awhile before I realized the pain that couples go through with infertility.

Some of the books say you should stop contact at age two or three, and Joyce and I can't understand why you'd do that. I went to their parents' 50th wedding anniversary, and I'm sure we will be in contact forever.

When we started the adoption process, we had no idea of the kind of relationship we would have because neither of us had any guidelines. It's been an amazing relationship that has really grown. They are so considerate, and they wanted to be sure I didn't feel pressured. We truly love each other.

Joyce — Ready to Adopt

We'd been married 15 years, and we'd discussed adoption several times. We learned early in our

*marriage that we had an infertility problem. I did get
pregnant several times, then miscarried.*

*We'd look into adoption periodically, and during that
time, things were changing rapidly in adoption. I feel
now that this was an advantage, and that we had worked
through a lot of things that have helped us be better
parents. We had worked through the grief at our infertility before we went to this agency. We were in touch with
Resolve and with Adoptive Families of America. We had
read, and we had talked with other people.*

*The next step for us was to decide on adoption or not
having children. We talked to people in both situations.
We knew we would be okay if we never had a child, but
we knew we would have regrets if we didn't try.*

*We realized parenting was important to us. We went
through training, first with the county, then with the
agency.*

Sensitive to Birthmoms' Feelings

*I had become very sensitive to the fact that birthmoms
are people with feelings, and I was concerned that I
might be taking advantage of someone else's pain so we
could have a child. The more we talked with people at
this agency, the more we felt their philosophy showed
respect for everybody in the adoption triangle.*

*They required us to go through three classes prior to
the home study. At one, an adoptive couple spoke about
their open adoption experiences. At the second, a
birthparent spoke, and at the third, an adoptee spoke.
After the speaker left we could talk it through with the
social worker. That was very helpful.*

*We know several people who are adopted, have no
access to birthfamily information, and are struggling
with searching. Openness relieves so many of those fears
of the unknown. In my mind, 30 years from now, our*

*relationships will be so intertwined that people will
think we are one family, and we are. We can't imagine
anything else now.*

*It's hard when you start that process in the home
study and it's not a real person. It's hard to believe
you'll be able to trust someone on this level. But when
we actually met and our relationship developed . . .
when we met, April didn't know if she wanted to continue physical contact after he was born. Gary and I
developed such a bond with April that we weren't sure
how we would deal with that.*

Time for the Interview

*When we met April, she had already interviewed
other couples. We knew that going into the meeting. I
tried to put myself in her shoes as much as I could.
When the social worker said she had interviewed other
couples, I thought to myself, "I would want to do that."*

*We had so much in common in our value system. I felt
like this was a person I would know was on my side as a
parent.*

*Of course at the first meeting we were nervous. I tried
to remind myself that this was not someone judging us.
This was someone trying to find people she could trust
to raise her child. I gave her the most honest answers I
could so she would know who we were. If we were not a
good match, she would know.*

*I was impressed with her questions. She asked ques-
tions about our relationship with each other, questions
about how our faith would impact how we raised our
child, questions about how we would discipline our
child.*

*I remember sharing with her who I was as a person
and also some real specific things that would help her
know Gary and me as a couple.*

Prenatal Visits Together

April invited me to go with her to the doctor. We started talking about what might happen at the birth and after the birth.

The first time we went to the doctor, she hadn't told them she was bringing me. She would say, "This is the mother." We talked with a nurse about some things that might happen in the hospital. I was there to hear the heartbeat. Then we went back to talk to the doctor.

This was the first time this doctor had been involved in adoption where you don't hide the adoptive parents from the birthparents. I told him I realized that she was his patient, and I was not. I told him that if she says now she wants me in the delivery room, but changes her mind at that time, it will be fine. I will wait outside. After we talked, he decided this was a better way to have an adoption happen.

Jon Is Born

April invited us to be there for the birth. We asked her if she wanted Gary there, and she said, "Yes. I want Jon to have that story of his birth that adopted children often miss."

We left for awhile during labor, and she called us back in just as the baby was presenting. There are not words to describe the birth.

She was in the hospital two days, and it was such a sweet time. We would come into her room, and they would bring the baby in. The nurse warned her about bonding with the baby, and she said to me, "But I already am bonded!"

She and her sister, Gary and I spent quite awhile in her room with Jon, each of us holding him, focusing on the miracle of his birth.

I did feel nervous about one thing. What if she

*decided to change her mind, would she be able to if we
were there? So I told her that if she decided to parent,
we'would accept that decision. She immediately reassured me. As much as she loved him, this was the decision she wanted to make. That for me was entitlement,
entitling me to be his mother.*

*Over the next few days I assured April I knew I would
never be Jon's birthmother. I wanted him to love and
respect the place in his life she held. I didn't feel threat-
ened that if he loved her, he couldn't love me enough.*

*We are in a one-sided correspondence with the
birthfather. We invited him to meet us both before and
after the birth and he declined. He didn't have the
counseling that she had. But we know who he is and he
knows who we are. Periodically we correspond and send
pictures.*

*We met April's parents soon after meeting April, and
then we all met together with my parents and Gary's. I
think if we had all met at a church fellowship dinner, we
would all be friends.*

We Discuss Our Future Together

*April and her sister came when Jon was a week old,
and when he was a month old. Sometime during those
meetings we started talking about what we would do
over time. We felt this bond, and that it would be a lack
of integrity if we didn't see each other any more. If at
any point it was a problem for Jon, cause confusion as
people said it might, we'd tell her and we'd decide what
to do.*

*My brother and Gary's brother started talking to their
kids about Jon's birthparents. They had no problem with
it. They know lots of kids who have several sets of
parents. So early on we realized we didn't need to put
that disclaimer on any more.*

Child Benefits from Contact with Birthmom

Contact with April is so beneficial for Jon. She has always made it clear that we are his parents, so we need to remember to invite her to spend time with us because she will never insist on it. I think now she knows, but in the beginning, we had to figure out a way to help her realize we weren't saying that because we thought we should. We really did mean it.

It takes a lot of pressure off me to know I can call April whenever I want, and she calls me. We have developed a relationship between us that is special on its own. Of course Jon is integral to this, but we care about each other as people, and that has been special.

We told April we wanted to meet her family. People warned her we would do that for a year or two, and then we would fade away. I said, "If you ever ask us to do something that we don't see we can, we will say so. We'll work it out from there. We have invited you into our relationship, and we are not going to disappear."

During the first few months after Jon was born, we laid that groundwork. At first April wasn't sure how she would feel about certain things. I had thought we'd have to write down exactly how much we would see each other. Then I realized that before birth she didn't know what she'd want. So I said, "I want us to feel that we are honestly communicating with each other. If you don't know how much contact you want now, let's wait and see."

I'm glad we were working with the agency because they could help with some of those issues once the baby was born. They were always completely honest. They also questioned me about not only what I wanted to say, but also what I needed to say.

Jon was two in January, and he's wonderful. April says this is the way it's supposed to be—and we agree.

Gary—"I'm a Dad at Last!"

When we got into our home study group, I realized they depend on those training sessions to help people understand the open adoption concept. The social workers say your chances for being able to adopt are much greater if you pursue open adoption. They work closely with the desires of the birthparents and of the adoptive parents. The training sessions helped to get us talking with each other.

We read about adoption, and one book was especially influential. The author was an adoptive mother, and she wrote about how she empathized with this birthmother and saw adoption through her eyes. I think this has helped Joyce and me to understand that there are other people, not just us, affected by this adoption.

Open Adoption Looks Better and Better

The more we talked, the healthier open adoption appeared to be. When we met April, we didn't know how open this would be, or how open we wanted it. The social worker implied that once the adoption happened, April wanted to continue only through letters and pictures. Once we met her, we knew we wanted more. It took some overtures on our part to demonstrate to her that we were serious, that we really did want her to stay involved.

Why openness? We felt it was the healthiest thing for our adopted child. We are all committed to that together. Once we met each other and knew it could work, we all decided she would stay part of his life.

Even now, at age two, Jon talks about April and her sister. We think this is real good for him. When he's an adolescent and is mad at us, and says, "I want to go live with my birthmother," we'll say, "All right, go call her."

The birthfather is another issue. We have made some

overtures, but have no contact from him at all. There are some life style issues there that we may not be as comfortable with as we are with April. But that may change down the road.

He has other children—Jon has siblings out there, which is one of the reasons we want to stay in contact with his birthfather. We're grateful that he signed the paperwork.

Jon's Birth—Incredible

Jon's birth was an incredible experience. It was a real gift that April gave us. Once you realize you aren't going to have biological children, you don't ever expect to go through the delivery of your child. One of the neatest things in that hospital experience was the morning Jon was born. We were in April's room, and Joyce hugged her and said, "Even though we're here, we want you to know it's okay for you to change your mind."

I firmly believe that if April had changed her mind at that point, we would have been fine with it. If we had felt we were robbing April of this little baby, we would not have been okay. I think we probably would have maintained a relationship with April and Jon.

When we got him home, it was the greatest thing. I took off work for a week. Nobody knew we were pursuing adoption except our parents. I even had some extra snow days.

The next day I prepared a little video tape. I was sitting in my rocking chair, and told the staff at school that I didn't want them to think I was water skiing in the Caribbean. This was my reason—and I picked up Jon. They were blown away. They had known about our last miscarriage, and they were very excited.

Jon has been the best thing that ever happened in our lives. I love being a dad.

Many books are available for adoptees and adoptive families. Far fewer have been published for and about birthparents.

The following bibliography includes the books mentioned in *Pregnant? Adoption Is an Option.* Also listed are other books dealing primarily with adoption from the birthfamily's perspective plus a few titles for pregnant teenagers, whether or not they are considering an adoption plan.

Price quotes are from *Books in Print,* 1996. Because prices change so rapidly, however, and because publishers move, it is wise to call your local library reference department for an updated price and address before ordering a book. If you can't find a book you want in your bookstore, you can usually get it directly from the publisher. Enclose $3 for shipping in addition to the price of the book. See page 224 for an order form for Morning Glory Press publications.

Arms, Suzanne. *Adoption: A Handful of Hope.* 1989. 320 pp. $14.95. Celestial Arts Publishing, P.O. Box 7123, Berkeley, CA 94707. 510/559-1600.

Arms explores changing attitudes in adoption and provides valuable insight into the longterm effects of adoption. She offers detailed suggestions that can empower everyone involved to create successful, humane adoptions.

Arthur, Shirley. *Surviving Teen Pregnancy: Your Choices, Dreams and Decisions.* Revised 1996. 192 pp. Hardcover, $17.95; paper, $11.95. Morning Glory Press, 6595 San Haroldo Way, Buena Park, CA 90620. 714/828-1998.
Helps pregnant teens understand their alternatives. Offers guidance in learning decision-making. Chapter on adoption planning is included.

Burlingham-Brown, Barbara, M.S. *"Why Didn't She Keep Me?" The Question Every Adopted Child Asks.* 1993. 169 pp. Hardcover, $19.95. Diamond Communications, P.O. Box 88, South Bend, IN 46624. 219/299-9278.
Narratives by birthmothers who candidly reveal the rational, practical, and emotional motivations that led them to place a child for adoption.

Colgrove, Melba, Harold Bloomfield, and Peter McWilliam. *How to Survive the Loss of a Love.* 1993. 212 pp. $5.95. Prelude Press, 8159 Santa Monica Boulevard, Los Angeles, CA 90046. 800/543-3101.
Daily affirmations, survival poems, and sayings for anyone who has lost someone special.

Connelly, Maureen. *Given in Love: Releasing a Baby for Adoption.* 1989. 24 pp. Paper, $2.95. Centering Corporation, 1531 N. Saddle Creek Road, Omaha, NE 68104-5074. 402/553-1200.
Could help a potential birthparent prepare for the separation from and loss of her child. Book also offers support during the grief she will experience, but implies the adoption is closed and she will not be seeing her child again.

Gritter, James L. *The Spirit of Open Adoption.* 1996. $18.95. Child Welfare League of America, Inc., 440 First Street, NW, Suite 310, Washington, DC 20001. 202/638-2952.
An account of an agency's reasons for switching from closed to open adoptions in 1980. Describes effects on birthparents, adoptive parents, practitioners, and, most important, the children.

Gritter, James L., Editor. *Adoption Without Fear.* 1989. 176 pp. $8.95. Corona Publishing Company, PO Box 12407, San Antonio, TX 78212. 210/341-7525.
Emotional, first-person accounts of seventeen families who chose to build their families through open, fully disclosed adoption.

Hicks, Randall B. *Adopting in America.* 1993. 144 pp. Paper, $13.95. WordSlinger Press, P.O. Box 53, Sun City, CA 92586-9998. 909/679-2661.

Book is designed to help prospective adoptive parents find a child, but the section on laws, listed by state, can be helpful to birthparents.

Johnston, Patricia Irwin, Ed. *Perspectives on a Grafted Tree*. 1983. 144 pp. Hardcover, $12.95. Perspectives Press, P.O. Box 90318, Indianapolis, IN 46290-0318. 317/872-3055.
A beautiful collection of poems written by birthparents, adoptees, adoptive parents, and extended family members.

Jones, Merry Bloch. *Birthmothers: Women Who Have Relinquished Babies for Adoption Tell Their Stories*. 1993. 316 pp. Paper, $14.95. Chicago Review Press, IPG, 814 North Franklin Sreet, Chicago, IL 60610. 312/337-0747.
Seventy women share their experiences of giving birth to a baby and placing that child for adoption. Most experienced closed, confidential placement.

Lindsay, Jeanne Warren. *Open Adoption: A Caring Option*. 1987. 256 pp. Hardcover, $15.95; paper, $9.95. Morning Glory Press.
Sensitive account of open adoption. Written for birthparents, adoptive parents, and professionals. Includes personal experiences of many birthparents and the adoptive parents they chose for their baby.

_____. *Parents, Pregnant Teens and the Adoption Option: Help for Families*. 1989. 208 pp. Paper, $8.95. Morning Glory Press.
Guidance for parents of pregnant teenagers, especially those considering an adoption plan. Offers practical suggestions for providing support while encouraging the young person to take responsibility for her/his decisions. Much of the book is in words of birthgrandparents.

_____ and Jean Brunelli. *Teens Parenting—Your Pregnancy and Newborn Journey*. 1993. 192 pp. Spanish edition, *Adolescentes como padres—Jornada de tu embarazo y nacimiento del bébe*. 1993. Hardcover, $15.95; paper, $9.95. Workbook for each edition, $2.50. Teacher's Guide for Spanish edition, $2.50. Morning Glory Press.
Prenatal health book for pregnant teenagers. Includes chapter on adoption. Also available in Easier Reading Edition (third grade reading level) with workbook and teacher's guide. Same prices as above.

_____, and Catherine Monserrat, Ph.D. *Adoption Awareness: A Guide for Teachers, Counselors, Nurses and Caring Others*. 1989. 256 pp. Paper, $9.95. Morning Glory Press.
A guide to talking about adoption "when nobody's interested." Good resource for people who work with pregnant women.

Mason, Mary Martin. *Designing Rituals of Adoption for the Religious and Secular Community.* 1995. 91 pp. $12.95. O. J. Howard Publishing, 4012 Lynn Avenue, Edina, MN 55416. 612/922-1136.
Birth and adoptive families can follow the suggestions, designing their own ritual, or picking from a variety of both secular and religious services.

_____. *Out of the Shadows: Birthfathers' Stories.* 1995. 270 pp. Paper, $14.95. O. J. Howard Publishing.
Puts to rest the idea that birthfathers are uncaring sperm donors escaping responsibility. A testament to the healing powers of openness in adoption.

Melina, Lois Ruskai, and Sharon Kaplan Roszia. *The Open Adoption Experience: A Complete Guide for Adoptive and Birth Families — From Making the Decision Through the Child's Growing Years.* 1993. 389 pp. $11. HarperCollins Pub. Ordering address: 1000 Keystone Industrial Park, Scranton, PA 18512-4621. 717/941-1500.
Authors offer detailed discussion of the many advantages and possible problems of open adoption. Helps adoptive and birthparents know what to expect as their open adoption relationship unfolds. Excellent guide to developing a satisfying open adoption relationship between birth and adoptive families.

Miller, Kathryn Ann. *Did My First Mother Love Me? A Story for an Adopted Child.* 1994. 48 pp. Hardcover, $12.95; paper, $5.95. Morning Glory Press.
A wonderful story for every adopted child. Contains special section, "How to Talk with Your Child About Adoption."

Partridge, Penny Callan. *An Adoptee's Dreams: Poems and Stories.* 1995. 56 pp. $10 ea. 6+, $6 each. Penny Partridge, 38 Cosby Avenue, Amherst MA 01002.
Mostly poetry with some prose, written by an adoptee who found her birthmother 20 years ago. Can help birthmothers better understand the feelings their birthchild may develop concerning the adoption.

Pierson, Anne. *Basic Decision Making,* 34 pp.; *Looking at Adoption,* 18 pp. $4.50 each. Part of the "Baby and Me" Series. Other titles include *Living Alone, Going Home,* and *Sharing an Apartment.* Loving and Caring, 1905 Olde Homestead Lane, Lancaster, PA 17601. 717/293-3230.
Workbooks written for women experiencing unplanned or crisis pregnancy. Recommended by "Alexis," one of the 39 birthparents interviewed for **Pregnant? Adoption Is an Option.** *Written from a Christian perspective. A secular version is scheduled for 1997.*

Roles, Patricia. *Saying Goodbye to a Baby: Volume 1—The Birthparent's Guide to Loss and Grief in Adoption.* 1989. 92 pp. $12.95. Child Welfare League of America, Inc.
Deals with birthparent grief after adoption and throughout life.

Romanchik, Brenda. *A Birthmother's Book of Memories.* 60 pp. 1994. $15.95. R-Squared Press, 721 Hawthorne, Royal Oak, MI 48067. 810/543-0997.
Lovely present for a birthmother to give her birthchild. Space for describing her early life, her pregnancy, and her adoption decision—plus a section for memories as the child grows.

Romanchik, Brenda, and Jim Gritter. *If You're Considering Adoption: A Guide for Prospective Birthparents.* 1997—In Progress. Write R-Squared Press for information.

Romanchik, Brenda, ed. *Open Adoption Birthparent.* Quarterly newsletter. 8 pp. $12/year. R-Squared Press.
Wonderful newsletter especially for birthparents in open adoption. Suggestions for interacting with birthchildren on visits as well as articles on grieving and other relevant topics.

Severson, Randolph W. *Dear Birthfather.* 1993. 13 pp. $6. Heart Words, 5025 North Central Expressway, Suite 3040, Dallas, TX 75205. 214/521-4560.
Good resource for birthfathers. Supportive and informative.

Silber, Kathleen, and Phylis Speedlin. *Dear Birthmother: Thank You for Our Baby.* 1991. 193 pp. $10.95. Corona Publishing Company.
A classic. Refutes such myths of adoption as the idea that birthparents don't care about their babies. Includes many beautiful letters from adoptive parents to birthparents and from birthparents to adoptive parents.

Silber, Kathleen, and Patricia Martinez Dorner. *Children of Open Adoption.* 1990. 193 pp. $9.95. Corona Publishing Company.
Authors show how love is multiplied and energies are used more productively when adoptive and birthfamily ties are open and not a mystery.

Stephenson, Mary. *My Child Is a Mother.* 1994. 253 pp. $8.95. Corona Publishing Company.
Adoption story from viewpoint of birthgrandmother.

Wolch-Marsh, Mary Jean. *Planning a Birthmother's Day Celebration.* 1996. 80 pp. $15. R-Squared Press.
Practical planning advice for the new holiday especially commemorating birthmothers. Includes suggested poems, readings and songs.

VIDEOS

"Using the A Word—Talking to Teens About Adoption." 1994. 45
min. $125. WACSAP, 172 20th Avenue, Second Floor, Seattle, WA
98122. 206/323-3926.
*Offers a realistic treatment of adoption for teens. Good overall discussion of
adoption including the grief and loss inherent in the process. Counseling
skills and openness in adoption are stressed.*

"Tough Choices: An Adoption Video." 1994. 38 min. $52.99.
Runestone Regional Learning Center, 817 Fillmore, Alexandria, MN
56308. 612/762-0627.
*Story of five teen moms and one teen dad who placed their babies for
adoption.*

"We Are Family: An Adoption Story." 1992. 24 min. $270. New
Dimension Media, Inc., 85803 Lorane Highway, Eugene, OR 97405.
541/484-7125.
*Story of high school students Ellie and Kurt who, after weeks of agonizing,
make an adoption plan for their baby. The baby is placed with the adoptive
couple, and the birthparents continue to be involved through letters, photos,
and visits. Video is a beautiful look at adoption without forgetting the pain
inherent in the loss of one's child to another family.*

HELPFUL ORGANIZATIONS

As you consider an adoption plan, the following organizations can provide additional information:

CUB Inc.
Concerned United Birthparents
2000 Walker Street
Des Moines, IA 50317
515/263-9558
Monthly newsletter. Local support groups in many communities. Call for information.

National Adoption Information
Clearinghouse
5640 Nicholson Lane, Ste. 300
Rockville, MD 20852
301/231-6512;
FAX 301/984-8527
(Contact for free adoption information sheets including list of adoption agencies.)

American Adoption Congress
1000 Connecticut Ave. NW, #9
Washington, DC 20036
202/483-3399
Provides support for all members of adoption triad.

Adoptive Families of America
3333 Highway 100 North
Minneapolis, MN 55422
612/535-4829
(Birthparent column included in monthly magazine.)

American Association of Open
Adoption Agencies
1000 Hastings
Traverse City, MI 49686
616/947-8110
Can refer families to agencies who practice open adoption.

ABOUT
THE AUTHOR

Jeanne Warren Lindsay developed the Teen Parent Program at Tracy High School, Cerritos, California, and coordinated the program for many years. She is the author of 15 other books dealing with adolescent pregnancy and parenting including the four-book *Teens Parenting* **series** used in many classrooms.

By the time her first book, *Pregnant Too Soon: Adoption Is an Option,* went out of print in 1996, 40,000 copies had been sold. Her other adoption titles include *Open Adoption: A Caring Option; Parents, Pregnant Teens and the Adoption Option: Help for Families;* and *Adoption Awareness: A Guide for Teachers, Counselors, Nurses and Caring Others* (co-authored by Catherine Monserrat).

Lindsay grew up on a farm in Kansas. She has lived in the same house in Buena Park, California, for 36 years. She loves to visit the Middle West, but says she's now addicted to life in Southern California.

Lindsay has graduate degrees in Anthropology and Consumer and Family Science. She and Bob have five children and five grandchildren.

Lindsay speaks frequently at conferences across the country, but says she is happiest while interviewing young people for her books or writing under the big elm tree in her back yard.

OTHER RESOURCES FROM MORNING GLORY PRESS

DID MY FIRST MOTHER LOVE ME? A Story for an Adopted Child. Picture book. Birthmother shares reasons for placing her child.

OPEN ADOPTION: A Caring Option. Discussion of the move toward openness in adoption—for birthparents and adoptive parents.

PARENTS, PREGNANT TEENS AND THE ADOPTION OPTION: Help for Families. For parents of teens considering an adoption plan.

ADOPTION AWARENESS: A Guide for Teachers, Counselors, Nurses and Caring Others. How to talk about the adoption option when nobody's interested.

SURVIVING TEEN PREGNANCY: Choices, Dreams, Decisions. For all pregnant teens—help with decisions, moving on toward goals.

TEENS PARENTING—Your Pregnancy and Newborn Journey. How to take care of yourself and your newborn. For pregnant teens. Available in "regular" (RL 6), Easier Reading (RL 3), and Spanish.

TEENS PARENTING—Your Baby's First Year.

TEENS PARENTING—The Challenge of Toddlers.

TEENS PARENTING—Discipline from Birth to Three. Three how-to-parent books especially for teenage parents.

TEEN DADS: Rights, Responsibilities and Joys. Parenting book for teenage fathers.

DO I HAVE A DADDY? A Story About a Single-Parent Child. Picture/story book especially for children with only one parent. Also available in Spanish, *¿Yo tengo papá?*

SCHOOL-AGE PARENTS: The Challenge of Three-Generation Living. Help for families when teen daughter (or son) has a child.

WILL THE DOLLARS STRETCH? Four short stories about teen parents moving out on their own. Includes check register exercises.

TEENAGE COUPLES—Expectations and Reality. For professionals, research involving survey of 3700 teenagers.

TEENAGE COUPLES—Caring, Commitment and Change: How to Build a Relationship that Lasts. TEENAGE COUPLES— Coping with Reality: Dealing with Money, In-Laws, Babies and Other Details of Daily Life. Help teen couples develop healthy, loving, relationships.

BREAKING FREE FROM PARTNER ABUSE. Guidance for victims of domestic violence.

Novels by Marilyn Reynolds: *DETOUR FOR EMMY* (teen pregnancy); *TOO SOON FOR JEFF* (reluctant teen father); *BUT WHAT ABOUT ME?* (acquaintance rape); *TELLING* (molestation); *BEYOND DREAMS* (six short stories about teen crises).

MORNING GLORY PRESS

6595 San Haroldo Way, Buena Park, CA 90620
714/828-1998 — FAX 714/828-2049

		Price	Total
Please send me the following:			
Pregnant? Adoption Is an Option.			
___	Hardcover: 1-885356-09-9	$17.95	_____
___	Paper: 1-885356-08-0	11.95	_____
Did My First Mother Love Me?			
___	Hardcover: 0-930934-85-7	12.95	_____
___	Paper: 0-930934-84-9	5.95	_____
___**Open Adoption: A Caring Option** 0-930934-23-7		9.95	_____
___**Parents, Pregnant Teens, Adoption Option** -28-8		8.95	_____
___**Adoption Awareness.** Paper: 0-930934-32-6		10.95	_____
___**Surviving Teen Pregnancy** Hardcover: 1-885356-05-6		17.95	_____
	Paper: 1-885356-06-4	11.95	_____
Teens Parenting			
—**Your Pregnancy and Newborn Journey**			
___	Paper: 0-930934-50-4	9.95	_____
___	—**Your Baby's First Year** 0-930934-52-0	9.95	_____
___	—**Challenge of Toddlers** 0-930934-58-x	9.95	_____
___	—**Discipline from Birth to Three** 0-930934-54-7	9.95	_____
___**Teen Dads** Paper: 0-930934-78-4		9.95	_____
___**Do I Have a Daddy?** Cloth: 0-930934-45-8		12.95	_____
School-Age Parents: Three-Generation Living			
___	Paper: 0-930934-36-9	10.95	_____
___**Will the Dollars Stretch?** Paper: 1-885356-12-9		6.95	_____
Teenage Couples: Expectations and Reality			
___	Hardcover: 0-930934-99-7	21.95	_____
___	Paper: 0-930934-98-9	14.95	_____
___	— **Caring, Commitment and Change** -93-8	9.95	_____
___	— **Coping with Reality** 0-930934-86-5	9.95	_____
___**Breaking Free from Partner Abuse** 0-930934-74-1		7.95	_____
Novels by Marilyn Reynolds:			
___	**But What About Me?** 1-885356-10-2	8.95	_____
___	**Too Soon for Jeff** 0-930934-91-1	8.95	_____
___	**Detour for Emmy** 0-930934-76-8	8.95	_____
___	**Telling** 1-885356-03-x	8.95	_____
___	**Beyond Dreams** 1-885356-00-5	8.95	_____
___**Video: "Discipline from Birth to Three"** 52 min.		195.00	_____
___**Video: "Your Baby's First Year"** 51 min.		195.00	_____
		TOTAL	_____

Please add postage: 10% of total—Min., $3.00   _____
California residents add 7.75% sales tax

                                          TOTAL _____

Ask about quantity discounts, Teacher, Student Guides.
Prepayment requested. School/library purchase orders accepted.
If not satisfied, return in 15 days for refund.

NAME _____ PHONE _____

ADDRESS_____